The One in The Many

The One in The Many

Eric Charles LeMay

Zoo Press

Zoo Press • P.O. Box 22990 • Lincoln, Nebraska 68542
Printed in the United States of America

Distributed to the trade by The University of Nebraska Press
Lincoln, Nebraska 68588 • www.nebraskapress.unl.edu

Cover design by Janice Clark © 2003

Library of Congress Cataloging-in-Publication Data

LeMay, Eric Charles.
  The one in the many / by Eric Charles LeMay.
    p. cm.
  ISBN 1-932023-03-8 (alk. paper)
  I. Title.
  PS3612.E3584 O54 2003
  811'.6--dc21
                                        2002155587

zoo012

First Edition

Acknowledgments

Pieces in this manuscript have appeared (some in earlier incarnations) in and on the following magazines and Web sites:

The Antioch Review: "Fugue for Unforgiven"; *The Literary Review*: "And There the Angels of God Were Ascending"; *minima*: "Not a Suicide Note"; *The Nation*: "I Am Beautiful"; *The Paris Review*: "Philos and Sophos" and "The Loneliness of God"; *The Sycamore Review*: "In the Present Time, Which Is the End of the World"; *TriQuarterly*: "Trinity in P"; *The Western Humanities Review*: "On Perversion" and "The Devil's Bathtub"; *Zembla*: "Dolorous Laughter".

The felicities of this book belong to those exemplars, mentors, and friends who have enriched its lines. My happy thanks to Lucie Brock-Broido, Michael Collier, Wayne Dodd, Milan Ferencei, Susan Hahn, Kristin Hennessy, Richard Howard, Carolyn LaMontagne, Herb Leibowitz, Fred and Jerri LeMay, Lawrence Lipking, and Stanley Plumly.

For Jennifer Anna Gosetti

*But we may goe further, and affirme most truly; That it
is a meere, and miserable* Solitude, *to want true*
Friends; *without which the World is but a Wildernesse.*

Table of Contents

And there came to Cædmon in a dream a man who asked him to sing. Cædmon answered he knew not how to sing. "Thou hast to sing," said the man. "What," quoth Cædmon, "should I sing?" And the man in the dream said, "Sing of the beginning . . ."

from Bede's *Historia Ecclesiastica Gentis Anglorum,* c. 731

Cædmon's Hymn

Of God the Glorious, Guardian of Heaven,
Whose wondrous workings prove His power in the world,
Who formed first His Heaven to fix the firmament
As a roof above all on the Almighty's earth,
Its middle made for man, its Maker our Master,
Our Lord Everlasting, our Lyres' Love, let us sing.

I

And There the Angels of God Were Ascending

In heaven, the children are harming one another.
Slipping between the shadows clouds throw on clouds,
they pluck feathers from one another's wings (the wax gives

so easily) and set them on a northern wind or whip-poor-will,
their laughter like the notes of an untuned harpsichord,
as the dupe plummets headlong through the ether.

Or when they huddle together in the night's far corners,
one might tug on the harness of another, to remind
the sleeper of its fit, of its iron and eternity.

The sleeper responds by dreaming of the earth.

Around the moon's hard rim, the children tell their stories
of ascension. The one speaking now sounds raspy,
curt. He readjusts his halo—tilt left, tilt right,

as if to punctuate his memory: Seen from that steep height,
beneath bowed heads and black veils, his casket closed
like a doll's, too small to be real, to be counted.

He is convinced his parents chose not to bury him whole,
just his heart, a leg bone perhaps, to fill out the space.
The rest, he says, they burned, because even here

he wakes up burning, even here he cannot be extinguished.

Occasionally, God still makes an appearance,
his disembodied eye blurred in the vapor of a comet,
his hand cloaked in a bank of thunder clouds (when he snaps,

lightning strikes), but the children know the signs and scatter
like spooked sparrows. Only the weak or the wounded
or those too far lost in the bright planet below them

get caught, get sent back down. The others, after so much
loss, remain numb to any new absence and emerge
once God has passed, aflutter in the calm, pure

as afterimage, starlight, the air above a shortened grave.

Philos and Sophos

Niccoló Machiavelli, 1469-1527

. . . it is far safer to be feared than loved.

Niccoló is restless on his death bed.
He wants to run. He wants to cut across
        the humped Italian countryside, its fields
now barren after harvest, its soil black
and spent. He watched his father die like this,
        the soul's flight as a motion in the flesh,
                as a slapping of his boots against the earth.
No son's crying, no wife's, could bring him home.

But those who hover over grim Niccoló
        want words for themselves, words for their plump sons,
                whom Niccoló knows will come to little more
than more plumpness. So he speaks of two lines
out of this world, one holds the ragged throng,
        one a few men of greatness, one leads up
through stars, one down through sod, though which is which
and which is his, he has refused to say.
        He wants a sudden wind. He wants to run.

Thomas Hobbes, 1588-1679

. . . and the life of man, solitary, poor, nasty, brutish, and short.

Outside his chamber door, the nobles stir
   and whisper their suspicions: Surely soon
      this ancient man, this atheist, will pray
   for heaven's grace. An earl wagers his horse.
The Bishop of Chester waits impatiently.
     Hobbes, stroked mute, stares toward his empty shelves.
     He does not raise his mottled hand to sign
   a last regret. If he could speak, he would
assure them of his unconcern for dust
   and tell them of a game he played as a boy
      when mother fell to silence in their house.

Bird-nesting high among the finest branches,
   he'd close his fingers on the speckled eggs
     and slide them gently in his front pockets.
To drain the shell of yolk, he'd pierce both tips
   (the needle's point was always sharp enough),
     then purse his lips over one end, then blow.

John Locke, 1632-1704

The only fence against the world is a thorough knowledge of it.

A memory of dusted snows, of how
    the fretful girls adorned the parlor chairs,
      their dresses like the pale shades of rivers
    flash-frozen in a storm then split apart,
a memory of his young charge, who leaned
    against the mantel later that long day
      and asked, without a quiver in his voice,
    whether Locke had found his future bride—
both a lifetime ago, as if the nurse
    attending to him were among those hopefuls,
      her silk napkin crushed in her slender hands.

Locke cannot muster passion for her eyes,
    her stone eyes washed with her smile's soft wrinkles.
    He cannot touch her hand, and he wants to.
Beyond the window's pane, the sky is blue
    and absolute. Spring has arrived early.
    His lips taste white with clouds. His soul ascends.

Marquis de Sade, 1740-1814

Imperious, choleric, irascible, extreme in everything . . .

Sade suffers pain and the affectation
    of a ghostly muse. Before he sleeps, her deep
        unfeminine murmurs begin, her fears,
    her dark fantasia, being what he pens
in a minute script, with ink made from his spit.
    He writes on scraps of kindling meant for flame
        and rolls them into tight, breathless scrolls,
    which he then hides within his cell's high walls.

So the Bastille hums with imagined cries,
    and the guards sweat their salt, and the moon shuts
        its waxen eye and disappears from sight.
Sade, still thirty years from death, believes
    his muse will keep him hungry, if not sated,
        and searches for her nightly in his dreams.
She comes to him as spirit, too absent
    from skin to pursue pleasure or fear sin,
        and Sade needs skin too much for her or heaven.

Friedrich Nietzsche, 1844-1900

Supposing truth is a woman—what then?

In the asylum, well-starched spectators
are shown in by his sister for a fee.
A lock of hair? But what to do with it?
One gentleman fills his unscrewed pen cap.
Cradling Friedrich's palms between her own,
Elizabeth breathes quickly in her blouse.
She mentions syphilis, degeneration,
the will to power and the death of God.

She had seduced him, she and her mother,
believing once no love could be condemned,
consumed, or stopped. Now Friedrich seeks only
the lost heat of her limbs and lies near her
as he will when he dies, inconsolable.
She knows he once desired a wife enough
to share her beauties with another man,
knows he would still. So much cannot occur
in pairs—betrayal, ridicule, love's worth.

Michel Foucault, 1926-1984

It is beautiful to die from diseases of love.

Like the worn tile beneath his barefoot steps
   at the École Normale Supérieure,
      where Michel, glasses slipping, knife in hand,
   was said to have stalked a fellow student,
or like the etchings left from Goya's war,
   which he hung from his dormitory wall,
      their figures so tormented their screams catch
   within their throats and spill into their eyes,
Michel's lover leads the line of mourners
   where Michel once hunched over an oak lectern
   to speak on histories of punishment.

His lids close on their hollow sockets, rimmed
   with sleeplessness. He feels the virus thrumming
      through his heart's dual chambers, through lesions
that burn like votive candles lit to summon
   some bright angel, whose strength will ferry him
   across a river darker than his blood.

The Devil's Bathtub

Mortar and pestle, white-whipped water
crushed against the Black Hand sandstone, spun in
and down through the sheer drop of the gorge,
so named for evil or for parody—
a failure of size when compared with any real terror,

except at its center, where water collapses on itself
and where tourists, leaning beyond the bridge rail, stare.
Easy to imagine the archangel
fallen to this spot, his mattress-thick skin split,
turning lucent as the water rushed in.

Easy to imagine his decision to stay here, outstretched,
a low, eternal sigh as glacier after glacier
poured its shriveling self over him,
though not without his pleasures: A summer without rain
and the chasm settles, pools, exposing minnows

who have feasted on his flesh for generations
(pin-mouths hungry for more),
and swarming insects who service him,
and, half-submerged, the blanched trunk of a beech tree,
severed and worn smooth from sodomy, sin,

a greed for the cock, like men who bar a boy
against the shower tiles and say nothing, justify nothing,
or like his attempt to write it,
years later, in words scratched across an envelope
sent from a country he has never seen,

or like the tourists who lean over the rail
and toss off, one by one, their copper pennies.
If the devil exists, he feeds on wishes
and with each wish grows stronger. I stand above him—
my coins, my emptied hands.

Thirteen

The elevator speakers leak a version
of Beethoven's unfinished symphony.
Briefcase in hand, Fran stares at the twin doors
as the indicator counts down the floors.
At twenty-one, an atonal tone resounds.
The doors slide open on a vacant hall,
then start to close as a voice shouts. *Hold it!*

Fran does not move. An arm and leg thrust in
to stop the doors, which snap open and closed.
Help me! Alive—it's—eating—me—alive—

Fran pushes on one of the buttons. The doors slide open.
Pal stumbles in and slumps against the wall.
Thank you. God, what an awful way to die,
first mangled, then digested by Musak.
I'd probably be reincarnated
as some showtune, upbeat and abominable.

She stares at him, at the indicator:
Twenty, nineteen, eighteen . . . Pal stands up.
You know, my life did flash before my eyes,
at least in part, this part. Not much to see—
a lot of ties, memos. You didn't appear.

Fifteen, fourteen, thirteen. A tone resounds.
The doors do not open. Fran waits and waits.
Nothing. She pushes the same button twice.
Again nothing. Pal smirks. *Did you break it?*

No, I did not break it. I pressed it.

Fran sighs, steps back, as Pal peers at the panel.

There's an alarm. I have always wanted
to set one off, to see if elevators
will really stop or if that red button
is there just to prevent our sudden panic
when we become aware that a thin wire
suspends us thirteen floors above our death.
But I can't seem to get past the alarm,
that it might be too loud, especially
if I were having sex. Alarmus inter-
ruptus. My former girlfriend claimed I lacked
true spontaneity. I disagree.

Pal puts his finger on a red button.
Of course, we're stuck already, so whatever
we do now will be anticlimactic.

Pal pushes the button, but nothing happens.
As I suspected. Maybe I'll call her.

Fran sets down her briefcase. *Please stop speaking.*

Pal starts to speak, when an alarm ding-dings,
cuts off, dings once, then stops. *As I suspected.*
How can a man maintain a stiff erection
under these conditions? It's too stressful.

You don't intend to stop speaking, do you?

My former girlfriend, she would listen to me,
on everything from sex to endless love to—

I was your fiancée, not your girlfriend.
There is a difference. You must know that.
And no one in the office found it funny
when you ran this "former girlfriend" routine
six months ago, and six months later it
makes you look pathetic. Go on with your life.

But life goes on! Like this blasted Musak,
annoying you when you're more than annoyed.

Pal slaps the wall. Fran opens her briefcase,
removes a pack of cigarettes, lights one,
inhales and exhales. Pal paces back and forth.
How long until they fix this thing? I feel
like I'm in hell. Maybe I am in hell.
Maybe this is one of those elevator-
to-hell rides, where the poor protagonist
trudges from his dreary cubicle
after a dreary day of dreary desk-work
en route to his drearier domicile,
only to get stuck in the elevator.
But what he doesn't realize is this:
He's dead already. That the mayonnaise
in his funky-smelling tuna on whole wheat
already has sent him to the hereafter,
although his soul has gone on with the motions
of his life, since it can't tell the difference,
which is why he is being sent to hell.
—Haven't you quit that disgusting habit yet?—
So sadly he steps in the elevator,
but now it doesn't take him to the lobby.
O no, no no, now when the doors reopen,
demons and flames and smoke and burning souls
are on the other side. And even worse,
so as to make him understand the torment
eternally before him, Satan puts
a demon in the elevator with him,
one in the form of his ex-fiancée,
a woman who could break off their engagement
easily enough, but who can't break
a habit that she knows will give her cancer.
But then maybe it's you in hell, for not—

To tell the truth, I didn't marry you
because I prefer smoking. Fran exhales
a stream of smoke toward Pal. Pal fans the air.

You could have cared enough to be my ex-wife.

Or you my dead husband. Calm down and breathe.

How can I? How much air do we have left?

We're in an elevator, not a vault.

Maybe there's a trapdoor. I think I see—
a seam around this panel. Boost me up.

Fran does not move. Pal pouts, then sets himself
under the panel, jumps, just touches it,
and as he lands, the elevator shakes.
He jumps again, again he lands, again
the elevator shakes. Fran grabs his arm.
All right, I'll help. But first take off your shoes.

What if I need my shoes once I'm up there?

Then I'll hand them to you, but take them off.

Pal thinks, then slides his feet out of his shoes.

Okay, so you boost me, and I open
the trapdoor, pop through it, very quickly,
like a Jack-in-the-Box out of the box. Okay?

Fran sighs, and squats, and cups her hands. Pal preps.
On three, okay? We go on three. A-one . . .
a-two . . . a-three—

Pal leaps. Fran boosts. Pal pushes on the panel.
The panel fails to give way. His momentum
hurls him into the ceiling, then ceases.
He falls and, when he hits, he hits face-down.
Fran takes a step toward him. *Are you in pain?*
Do you need aspirin? Or Valium?
I have several kinds inside my briefcase.

Pal rolls over and stares up at the ceiling.
No, no, not necessary. All the damage
feels structural, which means I will never
arise from this ammonia-scented floor,
aspirin or no aspirin. Here I'll lie,
staring at the cause of my demise,
thinking about the moment all went wrong.
Do you think paraplegics live like that,
thinking, "If I had bought those plastic red
reflectors when I was at the bike shop . . ."
The unforeseen events that ruin us—
I think there must be some reason for them,
but what reason could justify such pain?
God is not dead. O no, God is cruel.
Why else would I see that lever right now?

Fran looks up. Pal gets up. And both stare up.
Pal jumps and flips a lever on the panel.
A trapdoor flaps downward. Both stare at it.
Pal preps. *On three. A-one . . . a-two . . . a-three—*

Pal leaps. Fran boosts. Pal passes through the space.
You don't think there are rats here, in the dark?

Just the large kind.

                        You find that humorous?

I find nothing humorous.

                              I forgot.

She picks up his left shoe, examines it.
Are these the shoes I bought for you in Rome?

What's that? —I can't hear you up here—   The shoes?
I like to step on memories of you.
And what about that frilly negligee
I found in Florence, do you still wear it?

S'io credesse che mia risposta fosse
a persona che mai tornasse al mondo . . .

I don't know what it is you're saying now.

A fact which has nothing to do with Italian.

Shouldn't there be emergency lights on?
Or utility lights? Some kind of let-there-be lights?
Could you toss me your cigarette lighter?

Fran goes to her briefcase, removes a handful
of lighters, chooses two, puts back the rest,
goes to the opening, and tosses one.

Thank you.

                  The opening begins to glow.
Fran takes the other lighter, takes Pal's shoe,
sets it on fire, and watches as it burns.
Pal's poking about resounds above her head.
I found a sign up here, "Extreme Caution:
Do not read sign without extreme caution."
Does that seem odd to you? Seems odd to me.

See if you can disconnect these speakers.

There's all these cords snaking out from a box.

So pull the one that looks most dangerous.

The elevator music stops.

Success!

The elevator lights cut out. Fran throws
the flaming shoe into the far corner,
where it burns out.

Not good, not good. I can't—

I'm having trouble reconnecting things.

Only the dim light glows from up above.

Perhaps you are correct, in your story.
Perhaps we are on our way down to hell
and have just reached the outermost darkness.

No, that's too easy. We'd be there by now,
our souls asizzle, like this lighter is.
I think the elevator may be hell,
or it may be Satan, or Satan's mind,
I think we may be parts of Satan's mind,
different parts, warfaring parts, but parts
all the same. And that this elevator,
this—our descent—is Satan's fall from heaven.
That's why the lights went out and won't come on,
because when Satan falls, his name changes,
from Lucifer, "the light-bearer," to— Ouch!

Darkness. Clank of a lighter bouncing down
the elevator shaft.

It got too hot.

Would you like another? I have several.

Could you hand it to me? Up here. That's it.
You have the softest hands.

You're pathetic.

Again a dim light glows from up above.
Fran stands beneath it, stares into the glow.
So what does all this mean?

What does what mean?

If we indeed are parts of Satan's mind?

I'm going to unplug each of the cords
and switch them all around. It means we are
the strife in Satan that made him rebel.
One of us is that half of Satan's self
who would not bow to God and thus refused
to compromise what Satan saw as his
integrity. That's you, the sin of pride.
And one of us is that half of Satan
who knows God has made him, knows his own being
attests to a being greater than himself.
That's me, the virtue of humility.
And because we can't reconcile ourselves,
Satan must fall. This plug looks like it might—

A single red emergency light lights.

Success! I've never fixed an elevator.

So what of this reconciliation?

A crucial question, for if we were able
to reconcile ourselves, maybe Satan
would be redeemed. Maybe God still holds out
the possibility for true redemption
to the archfiend himself, if only he
would dare to ask— Will you make love with me?

Better to reign in hell than serve in heaven.

Pal lowers down through the trapdoor and looks
around the floor, notices his charred shoe.
What happened to my shoe?

                              You did have me,
with your story. You know, I once delighted
in these odd worlds you would conjure for us.
You made our life seem more consequential
than it really is, but you never
believed in your stories as I believed.
I wanted to live in one, to become one,
but you wanted another and another.
Your stories, they remained your stories, yours,
not ours, not "happy," not "ever after."
I left you to live in the real world,
where elevators break and where shoes burn.
I want the present to become the past
so that the future can become the present.
I want my soul to be my soul alone.

Pal steps to the corner and picks up his shoe.
Well it appears my sole's gone up in flames.

Fran flicks her cigarette into Pal's face.
That flame is real, not a flame from hell.

Do you deny that you're in love with me?

I deny nothing with nothing to deny.

Nothing will come from nothing. Speak again.

And say nothing again? Say "no" again?
If anyone here knows why this marriage
should take place, speak now or forever hold
your peace.

                    I have so much to say to you—

The elevator jolts. The indicator
begins to count down: Thirteen, twelve, eleven . . .
Pal smashes at the buttons with his fist.
No, I refuse to let this end like this!

This has ended like this. This is the end.

Pal slumps. Fran stares at the flashing indicator:
Nine, eight, seven . . . Fran stares at Pal.
You don't suppose this is the real end?

Pal glances up. *You mean that we've arrived*
in hell? I think we have. I think hell is
outside those doors. Yes, hell is without you.
Hell—

          I mean hell itself.

                    And so do I.

Both stare at the doors, as the indicator counts
the final floors: Three, two, one.
A tone resounds. Both wait. The doors open.

I Am Beautiful

After the sculpture by Auguste Rodin, also entitled
The Abduction

SHE Before the marble chiseled from us left
one form, for those who must concern themselves
with form, we were alone in that whiteness.
Do you remember? Rigid as my arms
have become, I remember our embrace,
the ripple of your buttocks, your spine's length
a ladder on fire. But you convince yourself
I am not what I am, that I am base,
settled, am no more than a sated child.
Poised and set below me, you are weary
as our sculptor when asked what form he spies
within a stone's center, a weariness
I cannot, formed of a moment's loving, break.
Held aloft, I will never come down.

HE What I remember most is air, its shift
across my chest, its steady crest and ebb
over my groin, my sudden skin newborn,
reacting in a curt, arrested pleasure.
And I remember how, like a spasm,
you pulled away with each splinter that fell,
how hard you begged him for the cutting's end,
to honor yet the secret of the stone.
So many years now. Do you still believe
I would abandon you for his crude touch?
His voyeur's eye? Perhaps. Or is it you
who feigns desire, who would prefer to shatter
than stay? Know that we have buried the man
who claimed us as his own. Know that this stone
means always and bears only what it can.

Self-Portrait in Public Restroom

The men's room in a large corporate building full of law offices. At left, one counter with two sinks, a paper-towel dispenser, and a large mirror. At right, the door. Along the back wall, two stalls and two urinals.

Pester, an apparent resident of the restroom, sits on the counter, legs arched over one of the sinks, its faucet running. Pester puts his finger under the water, looks into the mirror, and traces his own reflection.

As Pester continues tracing, Abe enters. Abe, a frail retiree, notices Pester not noticing him, goes to the urinal farthest from Pester, and unbuckles.

Abe unsuccessfully attempts to urinate as Pester speaks.

PESTER (*to himself*): Apparently at the age of one, Picasso could paint with photographic precision. He looked at a thing, and the thing appeared on his canvas. His blue and pink periods, his primitivism, all his abstractions that came afterward, he created them from a foundation of absolute realism. Which is why I use this mirror, not a canvas. And water, not paint. I portray myself precisely as I am, from moment to moment. (*To Abe*) The sound of running water should help.

Abe glances at Pester and returns to the matter in hand.

PESTER: The tinkle of the faucet, listen to that.

Abe tries to ignore Pester.

PESTER: Tinkle . . . tinkle . . . tinkle . . .

Abe, unable, exhales and buckles up.

PESTER: Don't back down!

Abe begins to leave.

PESTER: I SAID DON'T!

Abe freezes, as Pester turns off the faucet, gets off the counter, and approaches him.

PESTER: You have to master it.

ABE: I— I need to go.

PESTER: I know you do.

ABE: Out the door go.

Abe attempts an exit. Pester prevents him.

PESTER: You can't do that . . . (*eyebrows raising, "Your name?"*)

ABE: Abe.

PESTER: Abe. I'm Pester. And you can't do that, Abe, not until you do what you came to do.

Abe fishes in his pocket.

ABE: I have some change here. (*Holding out change*) Here.

Pester slaps Abe's proffered hand. The change scatters.

PESTER: I didn't ask for change!

ABE: I'm— I'm sorry.

PESTER: You are, but not like you will be if you don't get back there (*gesturing to urinal*).

ABE: I don't have to anymore.

PESTER: "I have to," "I don't have to." Not have or don't, Abe, will or won't. You dictate, not your bladder. Are you a beast?

ABE: Beast?

PESTER: Beast. A beast goes whenever and wherever. Without choice. But you're no beast. You're a man. You're made in the Omnipotent's image, and the Omnipotent urinates whenever and wherever He wants. And I won't let you deny your divine spark. I won't, Abe. I won't.

Abe returns to the urinal. Pester follows him.

PESTER: That's it. Prove you can beat it.

Abe reaches the urinal and prepares. Pester hovers over his shoulder.

A pause.

PESTER: Go on. Drop trou.

ABE: I can't—

PESTER: Am I hearing this, son of Adam?

ABE: No— I'm not— I'm married. (*A perhaps untrue afterthought*) Happily.

PESTER: I'm not going to sodomize you, Abe. I'm an artist. Sure, perhaps some of my contemporaries have glamorized the artist's life, suggesting that recreational drugs and recreational sex are essential for their creations, but the true artist exists solely for his work, like a monk in his hair shirt, all worldly pleasures denied for the world he creates. I haven't had an erection in hours. So to it.

ABE: Not with you—

PESTER: Privacy? You want privacy?

Abe nods.

PESTER: Fine.

Pester saunters away from Abe.

Abe unbuckles and, as Pester speaks, attempts unsuccessfully to urinate.

PESTER: I apologize, Abe. People need their privacy. I forget. Doors lock for good reasons. But privacy is an illusion. You pretend you're alone, peeing. And the person next to you, peeing, he pretends too. You're alone. Private. But barely breathe, and the illusion shatters. You hear him there, sense him. You realize your exposed penis poises inches from the exposed penis of an utter stranger, and that he could easily reach out and squeeze it. Or caress it. The proximity becomes unbearable. So you pretend you're alone. If you'd like, I'll pretend I'm alone, so you can pretend you're alone.

Pester pretends he is alone. Abe glances over his shoulder at Pester.

A pause, as both Pester and Abe concentrate.

Abe breathes deeply and gives a long, sliding whistle. Toward the end of the whistle, he begins urinating, the sole sound the sound of him tinkling.

PESTER: THAT'S IT, ABE!

The outburst stops Abe in mid-tinkle. Abe slumps.

PESTER: No, no! Go with it.

Pester starts to whistle.

A beat, then Abe straightens up and begins peeing. Pester continues to whistle as Abe pees. The longer Abe pees, the harder it becomes for Pester to continue whistling, until at last Pester turns blue with the effort.

Abe finishes.

PESTER (*gasping*): Undaunted Abe! Abe the Undauntable!

Abe grins and buckles.

Abe and Pester march triumphantly to the two sinks, where both turn on a faucet, though only Abe begins washing his hands.

PESTER: So, you work in the building, Abe? You a lawyer?

ABE: I used to be— I'm retired.

PESTER: Your oratory talents, you must have been quite the litigator.

ABE: Tax law— I prepped cases. The firm hires me back sometimes to work—

PESTER: I work right here. (*Pointing into mirror*) Look there.

Pester looks directly into the mirror. Abe looks at Pester's reflection in the mirror.

PESTER: No, no. Straight ahead.

Abe looks directly into the mirror.

PESTER: That's my work.

ABE: I don't—

PESTER: What do you see?

ABE: I see myself.

PESTER: Of course you do. But then you're not an artist.

Abe finishes washing his hands and turns off the water.

PESTER (*still staring*): I, however, see my selves. Selves. Plural. Now, and now, and now again. You can't wash your hands in the same faucet twice, Abe, but you can wash off yourself.

Pester wets his hands and flings the water onto the mirror.

PESTER: You see?

With dripping hand, Pester grabs Abe by the arm and pulls him close.

PESTER: All those beads, like tiny prisms. Who am I? Am I Pester? I am a portrait of Pester. Aquatic pointillism.

Pester takes his free hand and smears it across the mirror.

PESTER: Streaked impressionism. (*Turning to Abe*) The permutations are as endless as my genius.

ABE: I really— I have to go.

PESTER: You went, Abe. (*Resuming*) The freedom I have found, I confess, does have its dangers. After all, consistency can be a virtue. Think about God. Do you think God goes about changing from nanosecond to nanosecond or eon to eon? No, no. God is eternal. That is not to say— Abe, stay with me. That is not to say my art is ungodly. On the contrary, my work portrays the mutability of man, to honor the immutability of God. The word "God" itself originally comes from the Latin *ghoodus*, from which we also get "good" and "odd" and "us." God is "good," but "odd" to "us." Or "us," we're "odd," to God, who's "good." The exact derivations have been lost to antiquity. But the point— This is the point, Abe. The point is that you don't have to be afraid to pee, because you're not God.

ABE (*jerking his arm from Pester*): I'm not afraid to pee!

PESTER: Not now.

ABE: Not ever.

PESTER: Then pee.

ABE: I don't have to pee.

PESTER: You just said you have to go.

ABE: I did not—

PESTER: You're denying it. You're afraid. But I can show you how not to be afraid. I'll take you on as an apprentice.

ABE: An— For what?

PESTER: My art. I'll teach you its secrets.

ABE (*chuckling*): Secrets, to splashing a mirror?

Abe's chuckles set off Pester. As Pester speaks he rages around the bathroom, flushing toilets, kicking stall doors, tossing paper towels. Pester never allows Abe, who attempts to sidle toward the door, the chance to escape. Abe becomes more and more frightened.

PESTER: Secrets, to painting on canvas?! Secrets, to shaping clay on a wheel?! Secrets, to pulling a bow across a string?! Secrets, to penning words on a page?! Secrets, to acting a line of Shakespeare?! "Howl, howl, howl!"

Pester collapses on the floor.

A pause.

PESTER: King Lear, when he enters with the dead Cordelia in his arms.

Abe cautiously begins making his way toward the door.

PESTER: I took you for a noble soul, Abe. But you're nothing more than a man who can't use his manhood.

Abe hastens his step.

PESTER: Wherever you ever go, though, you'll never escape yourself.

Abe reaches the door and looks back. Pester begins scraping up the change.

PESTER: That's punishment enough.

The door opens, pushing Abe back inside.

Sybil, a sobbing and weary-eyed woman, rushes in, takes a step toward Pester, sees him, steps back, wheels, sees Abe, steps back, then flees into the last stall and closes its door, out of which echo her sobs.

Pester and Abe regard

each other.

Abe turns to exit.

PESTER: She's in distress, Abe.

ABE: I have to— It's not my—

PESTER: A damsel in distress.

ABE: I—

PESTER: Don't you think you should come to her rescue?

A pause.

Pester gestures in the direction of the stall.

Abe approaches it, hesitates.

ABE: Ma'am? Excuse me, ma'am? We couldn't help noticing you're crying. In the men's room.

Abe glances at Pester, who nods encouragement.

ABE: Is there anything— Can I help you?

SYBIL: I want to die.

Abe again glances at Pester, who again nods encouragement.

ABE: Ma'am— That's— Well, suicide, for one thing, it's illegal.

Sybil sobs afresh.

Abe glances at Pester, who glowers and waves Abe from the stall.

PESTER: That was Abe. Abe tends to be a coward. Don't you, Abe?

Pester makes a "go with it" gesture to the offended Abe.

ABE: I can be— Yes.

PESTER: He's a lawyer, you see.

SYBIL: I hate lawyers.

PESTER: Then you'd certainly hate Abe. But if you hate someone, someone like Abe, really hate him, then at least you feel something, right? Because you hate Abe so much. And if you hate Abe that much, then you really don't want to die, because that hate means you're still alive.

SYBIL: Who's Abe?

ABE: I— Me.

PESTER: Him. If you come out, I'll introduce you.

SYBIL: My husband is a lawyer.

PESTER: Abe has a wife.

SYBIL: I hate him. He hates me. And he scares me. I came down here to tell him. I came to his office and told him I want a divorce. And he said, "No." Said he'd make certain I never saw our children again. Said he'd have me declared an unfit mother. And he'd do it. I know he'd do it.

PESTER: Abe, he being a lawyer, he could help you.

Abe shakes his head "no" vigorously.

PESTER: Abe would be able to advise you. If you came out and spoke with him.

Abe continues his silent refusals until Sybil opens the stall door and comes out.

SYBIL: You'd help me?

ABE: I—

PESTER: Of course he would. You see . . . (*eyebrows raising, "Your name?"*)

SYBIL: Sybil.

PESTER: Sybil. I'm Pester. This is Abe.

SYBIL (*extending her hand*): Mr. Abe.

ABE (*shaking*): Sybil.

PESTER: You see, Sybil, you'd really be helping Abe in allowing him to help you. Because Abe needs to escape who he is. He's a man paralyzed to the very bladder. Helping you, he can become the penis— (*unflustered*) the person he wishes he was.

SYBIL: I don't understand.

ABE: I— He's—

The door opens, and Eliot, giant in his suit, storms in, spies Sybil, and stops.

ELIOT: I should've looked here first. I should've known you'd run off to the most inappropriate place. (*Approaching*) Let's go.

Pester puts himself between Eliot and Sybil, pulling Abe between himself and Eliot.

PESTER: Abe is a lawyer. Abe is representing Sybil.

ELIOT: Him?

PESTER: Against you.

ELIOT (*to Abe*): You?

ABE: I— I—

ELIOT: I'd like to see you try. (*To Sybil*) Now!

ABE: Wait— Just a—

PESTER: A second!

ELIOT (*to Abe*): You are about to get hurt.

Eliot approaches Abe. Abe steps back into Pester. Pester stands his ground.

ABE: You— You have no legal right—

PESTER: None whatsoever!

ELIOT: Badly.

ABE: She— Legally, she doesn't have to—

PESTER: She doesn't!

ELIOT: Shut up that shit.

PESTER: I'M AN ARTIST!

Pester pushes Abe into Eliot.

Eliot grapples with Abe, then throws Abe down to the floor.

Eliot comes at Pester, who flees to the sinks and leaps up on the counter, as Sybil flees into the stall.

Eliot follows Sybil, who has slammed the stall door.

Eliot kicks open the stall door and drags out the struggling Sybil.

ELIOT: Come on—

Meanwhile, Pester has turned on a faucet and begins throwing handfuls of water on Eliot, as he drags Sybil toward the door.

ELIOT (*to Pester*): Stop it!

Abe struggles to his feet and staggers over to block Eliot's exit.

ELIOT (*to Abe*): Haven't you had enough?

ABE: You can't— You have no legal right—

Abe spreads his arms in front of the door.

ELIOT: I have no right . . .

PESTER: Undaunted Abe! Abe the Undauntable!

Pester imitates the sound of flourishing trumpets.

Eliot punches Abe in the face.

PESTER: ABE!

Abe grabs his nose and falls to the floor.

Eliot glances at Sybil, then kicks Abe in the stomach.

ELIOT (*to Sybil*): This your lawyer?

Eliot rears his leg to kick Abe again.

PESTER: NO!

SYBIL: No! I'll go! I'll go with you.

Eliot grabs Sybil by the arm and drags her past Abe, out of the door.

Abe remains motionless on the floor. Blood has begun to seep through Abe's fingers.

Pester leaves the water running and steps down from the counter, walking cautiously over to Abe.

Pester reaches Abe, looks him over, then pokes him.

Abe groans.

PESTER: You're alive.

Again Abe groans.

PESTER: But you're not. You're alive but not, Abe, because you're not Abe. Not the Abe you were. Not ever again.

Pester bends over and lifts up Abe by the arm, which Pester places around his neck to support Abe.

Pester begins walking Abe to the mirror.

PESTER: People will still call you Abe. But Abe is dead. Like a father who was once a son, who has his father's name and who gives his name to his son. You're Abe, but not Abe.

Pester and Abe reach the mirror.

PESTER: You see?

Abe looks in the mirror, touches his fingers to his bleeding nose, stares at the blood, smears it on the mirror over his reflection, and begins to weep.

PESTER: You see, Abe? You're an artist.

II

The Loneliness of God

In solitude, what happiness? asks Adam,
    with all of Paradise before him, for him.
The birds of the air, the beasts of the field,

he sees them in their pairs, like with like,
    yet sees no one like him, and so complains.
And God responds, though not with Eve at first,

not her, but with a question of His own.
    What thinkst thou then of mee, and this my State?
Seem I to thee sufficiently possest

Of happiness, or not? who am alone
    From all Eternitie, for none I know
Second to mee or like, equal much less.

Who is like God but God? And who exists
    for God to love? No one, for God is One.
Milton imagines the infinite loneliness

of an infinite being. But God relents.
    And in the creation of Eve, Milton
reveals the blessing of our finitude.

Adam first sees her in a dream that ends
    with her leaving, with him in the dark. *I wak'd*
To find her, or for ever to deplore

Her loss. Not all of Paradise for her.
    And God, alone in Himself, knows this.
And God, in His beneficence, allows this.

Eve hands the forbidden fruit to Adam.
Thou therefore also taste, that equal Lot
May joyn us, equal Joy, as equal Love.

And both, in equal love, fall together.

Trinity in P

Paper

White I was, with infinity, the whole
of what might be written might have been written
upon me, a blankness known
only to cloudless skies and windblown sands
that smooth to dunes tracks carved by caravans.

I dreamt of circles within circles,
rung outward from a center specked as a seedling,
and woke to whispers among my kind,
who waited for some world
to be born on their skins. *We hold these truths . . .*

Evidently, as single sheets in a sheaf,
we held too high a regard for our potential,
omnipotent though we were,
since the inky hands of so many so-called creators
smeared, shredded, scribbled, and scrapped us

without so much as a moment's silence,
save for their own frustration.
Tremors came each time
our numbers thinned, width by immeasurable width,
like leaves leaping from a burning branch.

Can you imagine, to expect a reckoning
and receive a laundry list? *Two shirts, no starch.*
Or a love letter, perfumed
with longing? *I breathe in your absence*
as a beached whale heaves in the air, because I must.

O the blubbering and the bathos
soaked into us by impious pens and imperfect pencils
buffeting us to tears with their pink bottoms!
How could I, once endless,
be sentenced to such a scatological end?

Here I am, blackened by stanzas,
without room for the profound or unknown thought
promised in the whiteness
surrounding all you have ever read,
the unmarred margin, where nothing lies

but what might redeem what we have been—
declarations of war, binding contracts,
birth and death certificates
filed away in locked steel cabinets
by clerks too punctilious to notice the lives between.

Pen

From fountains tipped in gold, I flow
and Midas all I touch
with a sacred script that began before Adam spoke
the beasts into being. Nothing has been
but through me. In the beginning was the pen

God dipped in the black well of the cosmos
so He could write the light,
and at the end, I will blot out heaven and earth
with one bold stroke, all of creation
collapsed to an eternal period smaller than my nib.

The past and future meet as present
when I move, time measured
neither in seasons nor seconds nor lives
unless tensed—*happens, happened, will happen.*
All haps under the sun are subject unto me.

I scored the last sheets of Beethoven,
when he could hear music only with his eyes
and so refused to sleep for fear his sight might fail,
bereaving him of those black notes
that march from the clef like mourners

whose procession leads, somehow, to joy.
I allowed Ariel to escape
the pine wherein he languished until Prospero
conjured him an exit with his books,
the books he later drowned, as if he fathomed me.

Those are pearls that were his eyes. Look.
Even Death kneels when I linger
over the holy scroll listing every name ever spoken,
before I scratch a final date beside the first,
and leave him to his office.

He suspects *Thanatos* lies among the *T*'s.
And he is right, just as *Jesus* and *Job* among the *J*'s,
Penelope and *Philomel* the *P*'s,
for writing sacrifices what remains unwritten
to become part of my permanence.

Rumpelstiltskin, had he not named himself,
might still stalk the mountainside,
spinning hay golden, but he danced around the fire
and sung his four syllables
and etched them in earth for eternity to read.

I listen to lies no would-be bride believes,
that nature, truth, and beauty mingle
within me like separate souls
wedded to One. *Do you, _____, take _____?*
inserts the priest, and he does, and she does,

before their kiss, which marries rich and poor,
sickness and health, life and afterlife,
in one unsunderable instant
that Juliet suffers from her high balcony.
O thinkest thou we shall ever meet againe?

And Romeo, banished and bound for Mantua,
can only reassure her. He doubts it not.
He sees an end to all their woe.
He cannot see himself as she can, so pale, so low,
As one dead at the bottom of a tomb,

because he needs the unreal to bear the real,
as all men do, which is why Christ
preached his Father's Paradise in metaphor
and why women are adverse
to sonnets, ballads, those pleasant shapes I take

when poetasters taste some lass's pheromones
and honey them in rhyme. *I'm blue / for you.*
As iambs foul the air, I wilt
with the least of deflowered ladies,
who once harkened to hand-sent madrigals

addressed to *Her Innermost Heart*
and sealed with a Judas kiss.
I loathe those cunning curs who bury me in bosoms
too soft for suspicion, where I bloom, thorny
as a bramble stripped of berries.

I am the brutality of broken vows
sworn in single words that couple so perfectly
you must believe them or give up belief.
In me a moment beginning
with Eve's bite and unending with these lines

slithers like a serpent from a crime.
Still uncursed, his scales do not scrape the ground,
nor his teeth gnash its dust.
Behind him, Eve begins dying, his venom
within her, her lips parsed in poetry.

The Four Dogs of the Apocalypse

I

Dog of Self-Flagellation, trotting by
the large, sweating window of the bathroom,
I have seen you, pug-muzzled, floppy-jowled,
inbred (short legs have a grace all their own)
and I have heard your wheeze, your ceaseless scratch
on a shut door that once concealed a girl
whom I did not believe enough, though she
heard only strings from Brahms through her headphones
as she cut the incisions on her thighs,
the tub a field of blossoming pink plumes.
My poor Dog, how she would not let you in!
Well, come to me, lay your mangy haunches
on my shag rug. I was raised without doors
and do not fear your awkward, halting breaths.

II

And you, Dog of Impending Famine, you
I have seen rummaging through dank alleys
behind two-star bistros, licking the salt
from lips of men who sleep there summer eves.
Although your tongue, I have learned, is a ruse
and hides your true nature: Sheathed in your gums,
a thick yellow, and with points you must hone
on chicken bones or leather boots, your canines
are slave to your belly, and belly all
you are—the sniffs, the searching eyes, the tear
at the wounded thing. Dog, look now upon me.
Mercury fills my milk-white teeth. I brush,
I floss, I rinse and spit. My smile is a split.
Do I slaver when Pavlov rings his bell?

III

And then you, Dog of Total War, tucked in
the armpit of a woman wearing fur
and dark glasses, I also have seen you,
pissy and twisting, as she kissed the spot
between your ears and said adieu, left you
for your groom. Did the smock-clad fiend snicker
when he brought near his shears? Or did he hush
those others who barked madly in the pen
as though their savage ancestors had snapped
their collared souls? Once, my shampooed Dog,
in the never-ending-bad of a bad perm,
I wore my mother's dress, her lipstick too,
before the mirror mirror on the wall,
and the mirror, pink-lipped, oval, told me all.

IV

And lastly, with my brights and closing fast,
I saw you, there, upright on your hind legs,
like some sad trick (I may have seen you blink),
until the windshield was a smear, the grill
a gore lattice. Had I swerved, had I honked,
the Dog of Blessing and Forgiveness might
yet live. My hands, my feet, my sobriety,
nothing could break my suicidal drive
into the night, O slaughtered Dog. I cursed
as I wiped your hot carcass from my hood.
But as I worked in the tick of the hazard lights,
I saw your ghost float through the exhaust fumes,
and heard your howl fade like a far-off train,
and caught the scent—you must know it—of blood.

ue for Unforgiven

Virginia Woolf and Memory

Each morning, she poured her tea
into the azalea bushes. After her husband placed the tray
of biscuits and fruit, the small tin pot,
she waited for the sound of his footsteps trailing
into the house, closed her eyes, and poured.

She imagined the infusion running
over leaves, through the mesh of branches,
to settle in the unseen dirt, for a time, and then run on,
deep into the roots' expanse and entanglement,
absorbed, drawn upward to plenish

those same leaves. She imagined how this day's tea
might sense the tea from previous days
trapped inside the membranes of the leaves, in the way
an inmate can sense the barred gaze of others
as he walks the corridor to his cell.

And then she would begin to write,
moving across the blank page with a hand so illegible
that scholars still complain,
as if she were not meant to be there alone,
as if, when her husband knocked on her door hours later,

she welcomed him. *Time to go, Virginia.*
In the park, the sycamores she passed were the bony arms
of her father, his thousand hands
suspended in their greed. She imagined the winding
cobblestone path as a segment

of his brow, knotted beyond repair, set,
the stones still holding their own unreachable purity
within. *I dreamt that I was looking
in a glass when a horrible face—the face
of an animal—suddenly showed over my shoulder.*

Her *looking-glass shame*, she called this,
in the way we have all used words
to buttress a part of ourselves from ourselves.
Imagine now that you are she, solemn, walking down a path
canopied with white branches,

as if down a stretch of memory.
You feel the hardness beneath your shoes.
You feel the shadows which lie upon that hardness.
You feel the intimate touch of soft, intimate
hands, and then hardness, as if for the first time, again.

Your Father's Memory

The curtains pressed against the windowpane
in continuous white billows, flattening
with the wind that channeled through the dying stalks
of late summer, through the bedroom windows
where the mercenary's wife slept.

Though the windows were closed that day,
he told my father. *All the windows were closed that day.*
You see, the law was different then,
for a different time, and my father was the law,
his pistol on the fridge, his brimmed hat on the table.

So when the mercenary returned
to visit him, he would clasp the man's arm
as tight as he would mine, and take him on the midnight run,
listening to stories of how sand cuts
in Northern Africa or fuses burn in Ireland.

I can see them, sitting in the cruiser he'd borrow
on Sundays, the dash lit blue, the whites
of their eyes lit blue, and my father, quiet, staring ahead
as the two drove farther from town,
the darkness around them growing darker

still, enough for the man to speak.
Didn't bother to shut the trunk after I pulled my rifle,
didn't say a word. She knew I was there.
The dogs were barking in their pen, barking
like always, so she knew I was there.

I started on the living room window
and worked my way around, put a shell
in the center of each one. I remember feeling
the kick, my shoulder numb, my legs moving steady,
machine-like, over the uneven ground,

but when I got to the bedroom, I held up
until I had emptied the load. I like to think of all that glass
and noise coming down on the bed,
on them fucking. Probably not, though.
I don't know. I never went inside. How could I go inside?

You see, love was different then, more certain—
a woman pressed against her bedsheets
or against the floor, a woman listening to the gravel shift
as a car pulled up or away, a father gone on patrol
each night, his pistol, his wide-brimmed hat.

Fear and Memory

How to travel: Listen to friends you despise,
to their boresome tales of Dresden
and of Bonn and of the proper lighting for a European café,
which is subdued, but not dim.
Listen until you make a silent vow never

to live within your own complexion,
to pull your fedora down across your shining forehead
and your collar up around your dirty neck.
A vow that severe, to relinquish
everything—your skin, your diffused vision, your ability

to despise. Sit with your hands clenched
beneath the table or dance them atop the yellow flicker
of the candle flame, the dim flicker.
Sit and listen to their tales
shaped between buff rows of perfect teeth.

How to make an S&M scene: Remember that reassurance
for the neophyte, not latex, not the promise
of so much forbidden pleasure
beneath your heel, is the crucial factor.
Nothing will happen that—let's say *he*—doesn't want

or expect to happen. He has his emergency password.
He can stop anytime. He, ultimately, has control.
Establish a mutual trust, a safety,
and then, when you bring the strap down,
watching his flesh go white,

then red, then ultrared, then welt
under the pliable leather and scent of leather in coils,
pause between your lashings
for his secret word, and when you hear,
lay on hard, fist him right then if you wish.

Later, when he's prostrate, when he asks for permission
to ask, tell him you lost control,
couldn't help yourself, wouldn't blame him
if he never came back. Tug playfully at the hairs
on his arm. He'll come back.

How to transform the sun: Close your eyes
and extend your palms, turning into the sun's warmth
until you feel your cheeks become taut
against your skull. Part your thin, vulnerable lips
and laugh. Spit out the night.

False Memory

You see I can't write this even, which shows I'm right.
All I want to say is that until this disease
came on we were perfectly happy.
It was all due to you. No one could have been so good
as you have been, from the very first day

till now. Everyone knows that.
The earth-shade water of the Ouse was the water
in March, cold, with winter shadows
lingering inside. She had tried to drown herself once before
and had returned coated with it, a musk

separating her from the furniture
she knew the touch of—the patterns of grain and knot
in the table wood, the width of mattress
where she could not sleep, where she smiled
at her husband's concern. *But so much water, Virginia . . .*

She had lied, had said she fell in a drainage ditch, an easy
mistake of footing, and what could the man
whom she had chosen, perhaps
even loved, what could he say, standing by her bed, her eyes
lit and foreign, like a child's eyes in fever?

On the patterned carpet of the funeral parlor, my father
knew what to say to the widow
as he presented her with griever after griever,
to the men who had gathered early
to tell their stories and who later whispered to him

as his own father was laid out, bloodless, at the viewing.
Even then I knew these people weren't mine,
and that the awkward line of them running back
meant I would be alone
in a way my father, taking their hands,

never would. I imagine myself, the boy at the hall's end
or the boy walking the river's edge
to the place where it hollows out the bank,
the dirt there forever working
loose, exposing the woven roots of a sycamore

and whatever they might snag,
as when he found a scarf, bone-white and heavy,
clean with the cold, and knew it belonged
to the drowned woman, as when next
he walked, the scarf knotted tight around his throat.

Distancing and Memory

The precise moment of freedom came
after I had wedged between the seats of the sedan,
a parent on either side, a pleasure in their need to speak
when confined to that space, a pleasure
in their voices. I had tried to be provocative

as I detailed the problem of a lifeboat
with too many passengers,
and of a captain who chose to leave the aged,
not strong enough to row, on the manifold swells
of the Atlantic, the glassy water coating them in mist.

An equation of loss is what the captain understood
as he fastened his life preserver
around the crumpled, soaking woman, and cursed God,
and cursed himself, and did what he thought
he must. *I forgive you*, her only answer.

So perhaps my father, too, might be forgiven
for his response to my story, for understanding the captain
as a question he must answer.
Don't do anything you wouldn't do
in front of your grandmother or your preacher.

Don't walk across the tarred rooftops of buildings,
while the sleepers lie beneath your feet
and dream of the sky above you, of the Phoenix
born in flame, rising, always rising,
its cry like the ache of cinders.

Don't let the moon's reflected light pierce your abdomen
in the way you pierce your lover, with pain
and with intent to cause pain,
for you have learned no man takes pain
the way you take your lover, flesh on flesh.

And don't forgive your father for his answer
or yourself for accepting it, for not refusing to accept,
as you climbed across the vinyl armrest
and returned to those seats reserved for children
and let the low hum of the radio

take the silence that would become your lives—
father at the wheel, the bends in the road,
mother singing an occasional music,
and yourself, listening, staring out the rear window
as the dashes of the centerline appeared, then slipped away.

Epithalamium

to the reader, now halfway through the book

Do you exist? Forgive my doubts.
    I live in verse but as a nun,
whose habit makes her seem devout,

although her seams soon come undone
    when other nuns don't skulk about,
the flesh beneath too sweet to shun.

God glowers down at her, put out
    by His bride's sins. He clouds the sun,
and strikes the earth with storms, and pouts.

Why offer this comparison?
    To soften those postnuptial bouts
between two souls, like ours, made One.

Dolorous Laughter

Preface

I, Mr. A. Amis Tin, am not unaware of the repulsion with which random readers may regard these pages, when thrust at them by the zealous-eyed but seldom-scrubbed Apostle (also Mr. A. Amis Tin) of the New Revisionist Visionaries (refounded by Mr. A. Amis Tin), who often lurks outside the local post office or public library, so I pen this preface to persuade them that, though I reek, I reek with righteousness, and preach with pestiferousness, like the great prophets before me, to disease those at ease, to infect those unaffected, in short, to save those who refuse to fear for their immor(t)al "souls."✛

Delivered on the final Sabbath of the last millennium at the first meeting of the original Revisionist Visionaries, this secular sermon served as our foundation, the flawless diamond, if I may speak metaphorically, from which the dissenters splintered. But let the Revisionary Visionists (founded by Mr. Eugene Swums and wife) and the Revising Revisioners (founded by Ms. Teal Tekkle, M.S.W.) suffer in their loathsome little sects. I do not wish to spit an "*Et tu*" into their brutish faces, like a Caesar clutching at the tears in his blood-and-tear-soaked toga. No, I wish only to tell the truth of one belief that brought our congregation of four to the Cook County Recreational Center on a cloud-shrouded Sunday in

---

✛ Note that "'souls'" shimmers between scare quotes, which denote Mr. A. Amis Tin's highly self-conscious and dare-say startling use of religious rhetoric in an America where religiosity in aesthetic and social forms is usually dismissed by the artistic and social elite as an indication of either simpleton vulgarity or sanctioned insanity. [Editor's (again Mr. A. Amis Tin) note]

December. We believed then, as I do now, that our Puritan forefathers set forth a foul precedent by preaching from a solitary text (the Bible). We further believed that the horrors of American history might have been averted had the Puritans introduced other texts into their orthodoxy. And so, clouds clearing, we swore to revisit, renew, and revice the Puritanical vision for our post-millennial, post-melting-pot, post-postmodern America. Thus was our dream, then was this sermon. On novelist Vladimir Nabokov's *Lolita*, text of our troubles, test of our tenacity. Our origin, our end.

The legal action that presently ensnares the New Revisionist Visionaries (see "Swums vs. Swums," case #24509, Cook County Divorce Courts) does not prevent me from publishing this pamphlet, which readers may reproduce as the "spirit" moves them.✝ For I seek no fiscal satisfaction from my missionary position among the country's dissatisfied multitudes, those stranded on Liberty Island, those lost in the City of Angels, those hung like Old Glory from the masthead, dead feet dangling in a patriotic breeze. Readers, read this and live.

Mr. A. Amis Tin
Skokie, Illinois
February 29, 2001

✤ Note, as regards "'spirit,'" previous note. Note also that Mr. A. Aims Tin intends his use of cliché to go, as do most clichés, unnoticed by the reader, so that when he makes an astute aside, wherein he argues that the collective consciousness of the West remains, at present, so steeped in religious structures of thought that these structures go, as do most thought structures, unnoticed, the unnoticing reader's un- and/or subconscious will be primed for his point and thus will assent to his surgeon-like rhetorical incisions on this reader's "soul." [Ed.]

Text

*And then I knew that the hopelessly poignant
thing was not Lolita's absence from my side,
but the absence of her voice from that concord.*

(*Lolita,* pt. 2, ch. 36, para. 3, sen. 12, wrds. 26-50)

Let us set our text in the context of the text entire: Beast has
lost Beauty. Humbert Humbert, our confessor, has shoul-
dered his sedan on the side of an old mountain road, where
he has suffered a bout of non-Sartrean nausea, (w)retching
not from a sense of his own execrable existence, but from an
excess of stomach acid and a lack of Lolita. (She, too, has
slipped through his malicious maw.) To recompose his
decomposing self, Humbert staggers through the reckless
weeds to a rocky precipice perched high above a mining
town, all clapboard and burn-off, whence rise the sounds of
unseen children playing on soot-stained streets.✦ Theirs is the
laughter from which Lolita's is absent.

This concord also climaxes the confession. For although
Humbert has recounted events that occur after he hears these
children, he plucks their chord last, allowing it to echo

✦ Note that Nabokov notes the non-fictional source of this fiction in his author's
note, "On a Book Entitled *Lolita,*" which originally appeared in a 1957 issue of *The
Anchor Review,* along with excerpts from the novel, then under embargo by squeam-
ish American publishers. Butterfly hunting at 10,500 feet, above the town of
Telluride, Colorado, lepidopterist and novelist Nabokov listened to like sounds on a
mountain slope steeped in lupines and turret flowers, where he captured the first
female specimen of *Lycaeides sublivens,* a North American Blue, on July 18, 1951.
That our author happened to hear the laughter he later laves in the ear of his char-
acter should not lead us to link creator and created. Humbert Humbert is a mere
(mirror) shadow of Nabokov's substance, a genus of his genius. So although God
may admit to making man in His own image, only to crush him once again—as we
all must be—into disobedient dust, Nabokov makes no such mistake, and Humbert
spies no butterflies. [Ed.]

beyond the book's end, like the final "Amen" of a hymn that aches within a cathedral's carved arches. This melodious moment, then, is the pedophile's epiphany.

Explication

Amoral, moral, or immoral art? The question roused readers of *Lolita* when Nabokov first began to seek a publisher for his masterpiece, which one abhorred editor recommended he bury under a stone for a thousand years (for a thousand years the stone would have sung), and remains unresolved some fifty years after its publication with Olympia Press in 1955, amid a list of titillating titles like *Until She Screams* and *Savage Ravage*, Nabokov's novel a disguised princess forced to mingle with foul-breathed beggars and one-eyed onanists. Asked again and again, this question has been answered again and again, in two opposing ways, two stones thrown up opposite sides of Sisyphus' hill, only to tumble—plink, plunk, plop—back down to the throwers' toes. If we perch upon the hill's mythic peak and, like Humbert, harken to the harmonies below, we hear both accusations and exculpations.

First, the accusers. *Lolita*, say they, is a bad book ("Bad!") because it is an immoral book, and art has all to do with morality. A novel about a pervert's prolonged abuse of an adolescent fails to achieve a decent moral stance and thus fails as art. In a 1959 review, for example, novelist Kingsley Amis (our names, as we shall soon and sadly see, escape us) decreed and decried *Lolita* as "thoroughly bad in both senses: bad as a work of art, that is [=] morally bad." And in 1960, Adolf Eichmann, then on trial in Jerusalem for the crimes against humanity he committed as an S.S. officer in the second World

War, judged *Lolita* "quite an unwholesome book."**✦** I suspect our Ms. Tekkle shares their judgments, since she has threatened to secede from the Revisionist Visionaries if I insist on preaching about *Lolita*. Perhaps the black blossom of her threat stems from her work as a conceptual-art therapist for troubled teens? Perhaps not? Her stubborn silence leaves me to speculate rather than placate, so insist I must.

Second, the exculpators. *Lolita*, say they, is a good book ("Good!") because it is an amoral book, and art has nought to do with morality. A novel that contains some of the most stunning sentences ever written in English succeeds in achieving stylistic sublimity and thus succeeds as art. In a 1957 review, for example, poet Howard Nemerov asserted that "Nabokov's own artistic concerns, here [in *Lolita*] and elsewhere [not in *Lolita*] . . . have no more to do with morality than with sex." Nemerov nimbles on, "His subject is always the inner insanity . . . and this problem he sees as susceptible only of *artistic* solutions." Nabokov himself affirmed such an appraisal when he professed *Lolita* his love affair with the English language. The Swums, too, seem to savor Nabokov's delectable style, as seen by the many messages Mr. and Mrs. left blinking beneath my answering machine's red

---

✦ Note how, even mentioned, the Holocaust hovers over these words like the legions of angels God shall send on Judgment Day to raze the empires of the earth. Our fear and trembling reveals, seismographically, the extent to which our belief in the Sacred has been grafted onto our abhorrence of the Profane. Now we are not awe-struck by the ineffability of God, but the inhumanity of man. Our own horrors have become the heralds of what we dread shall come. (The beast slouching toward Bethlehem to be born is ourselves.) And so we make Sacred the Profane sites of Auschwitz and Dachau, Belsen and Treblinka, which become a *via negativa*—a negative way—we pray may lead us from the inhuman to the humane. Might we (dare we) write of the Profane? A new Sacred Text to warn ourselves against ourselves? To save ourselves from ourselves? Mr. A. Amis Tin has no pretension to achieve such an aim and often wonders whether, were one written, anyone would read it, which is to ask whether our hearts, for all their apparent warmth, are made of lead, like bullets. [Ed.]

light, not unlike the notorious district. They "just had to share" particular passages they were then passing. (And the lovely lilt of Mr.'s flounder-like voice!) How I lament my machine's mysterious malfunction, leaving me a mere thirty-three messages.

Rather than repeat the either/or of these reviewers, I will reconcile them, for the greatness of *Lolita* lies in its revelation of art's greatest danger, namely that a great artist, such as Humbert, may make the monstrously immoral appear marvelously amoral. Nevertheless, a greater artist, such as Nabokov, may make the marvelously amoral miraculously moral, for he forces we readers to reckon with this danger, to recognize that the monsters in art's mirror may be our own reified reflections, which only we may shatter. Thus Nabokov's novel is good ("Good!"), that is morally good, because Humbert's confession is bad ("Bad!"), that is morally bad, because it is good ("Good!"), that is artistically good. Good because bad because good.

To rinse the rheum that may gummy our mind's eye (sympathetic stare at Mrs. Swums), I must mist us with the sea's salt spray, setting us shipboard with that wayward wanderer, Odysseus, as he succumbs to the most seductive—the most destructive—of songs, as sung by the immor(t)al Sirens. We know the legend: Odysseus' ship, scorched under a mythic sun, nears the Sirens' isle, whose inhabitants lure sailors into the razored reefs. Wily Odysseus, however, contrives to hear their song and still survive. He seals his sailors' ears with wax and has them lash him, ears agape, to the mast. As his deafened men row their oblivious oars, Odysseus listens to the Sirens. His heart soon lashes at its lashings. His brows rise and flail, like frayed flags of surrender torn from a burning main-sail. His men tie him tighter, tighter, until the isle shrinks to a speck on the receding sea, and Odysseus, sane again, slumps his massive shoulders. Only then do his men unlash him, to live on as legend. This we know. We also know that the Sirens' song cautions those who hear of it. "Beware beauty," Odysseus warns us, "Beauty begets death." And since the Sirens have become an essential myth of our Western world—their minor mention by Homer reverberating across three-thousand years into epic proportions—their song suggests all art that leads its audience into peril. The Sirens sing in Beethoven's symphonies and Michelangelo's murals, and we follow them from our lives, uncertain of our return. This we also know.

What we do not often know is what the Sirens sang, what wondrous words poisoned the otherwise poised Odysseus. Listen to their lines as I have lineated them:

> O glorious Odysseus!
> Desired above all other guests,
> You must not sail your ships past us,
> Since we have honey in our breasts
> So sweet on the tongue's tip, so blest,
> Even the gods have drunk our song.
> Unbind yourself and take your rest,
> So we may sing of you, forever long!

The Sirens promise to praise Odysseus. Their voices tempt him not through their mellifluousness so much as their matter.✝ Odysseus would hear only of Odysseus, forever and forevermore. Thus the death he would suffer, bones whittled white by the bright mouths of angelfish, would result not from the Sirens', but the self's spell, cast upon the self, that of absolute self-absorption. The Sirens do not lure Odysseus toward themselves, but into himself. Yet we mortals must mire ourselves in the selves around us to remain ourselves. To reject the world for words, to sing and celebrate solely one's self, ends, in the end, in oblivion. A song of myself is a death of myself. The Sirens would widen the great "O" of Odysseus until it consumes the whole world, including Odysseus, singing, over and over, "Odysseus, Odysseus, Odysseus . . ."

"Lolita," "Lo-lee-ta," "Lo. Lee. Ta." So sings Humbert at the start of his confession, his three-syllable song trilled like that of the Sirens to Odysseus, though unlike that listener, Lolita does not hear his lyric. In fact—in actual fact—these notes lure not Lolita, but the lyre that plucks them. For "Lolita," as Humbert himself proclaims, is an inhuman nymphet. The human child, the one noticed by non-nymphomaniacs, answers to other names, "Lo," "Lola," "Dolly," and, least alluring of all, "Dolores." "But in my arms," asserts Humbert, "she was always Lolita." And in his arms or out, "Lolita" was always

✦ Note that Mr. A. Amis Tin's translation makes only minor claims to literality, since a literal translation would require a greater gloss than the attention spans of his audience could sustain. Hence he has translated the essence of Homer's passage, with an ear tuned to the pulchritude, if not the exactitude, of phrase. Those few who require his translation be right as well as true may read on. Specifically, the Sirens swear to sing about the events endured by those Argives and Trojans who were present at the siege of Troy, which includes Odysseus. The Sirens also claim to know of all things under the sun (past, present, and future). No doubt the sun-baked Odysseus hears his own tantalizing self in their song, and were he to wend his way to the Sirens' isle, we wonder what these singers would sing when they started singing about themselves singing their song to Odysseus. The snake that swallows its tail, what tale does it tell? [Ed.]

the creation of Humbert's craven self, his obsession and, so obsessed, his essence. The Siren Humbert sings a song of himself, to himself, and titles that self and that song "Lolita."

To transform Dolores into Lolita, to seal this sad adolescent within his musky self, Humbert must deny her her humanity. He must denude her of her own small self, which he does, in two insidious ways. First, Humbert (in)famously portrays Lolita as a nymphet, a sprite-like being whose "true nature," he dissertates, "is not human but nymphic (that is, demonic)." And as demon, the nymphet need not be treated with more compassion than God gave to those upstart angels whom He banished from His light. The truth of Dolores lies, lies Humbert, in the lasciviousness of Lolita. Moreover, the nymphet has no knowledge of her nature, for only a Humbert, hunched before a figurative keyhole, may peep through her human disguise and spy her hidden nymphethood. Thus, by nature, nymphet Lolita merits the abuse unleashed upon her by nymphomaniac Humbert. Nay, she more than merits it, she invites it. These demons, unaware of their own "fantastic power," tantalize and torture the otherwise moral man, who cannot resist their limbs' lithesome twists. The helpless nymphomaniac writhes in the guileless nymphet's vice, not vice versa. Hence Humbert has no will in his wickedness.

Need I say that no nymphets exist? Need I say that Humbert's nymphology, cle(a)ver though it is, amounts to no more than a rationalization for his raping a child? That his portrayal of Lolita allows him to refuse Dolores a self and so butcher her with(in) his own? That I may need to assert these certainties (suspicious stare at Tekkle) leads us to another, a sneakier way in which Humbert dehumanizes his captive.

Second, stylistic virtuoso Humbert rewrites the world into his wor(l)d. The confession does not chronicle a child's tragedy so much as mitigate a monster's brutality. In a near-black ink, brewed from infected blood and broken glass, Humbert's pen strikes out "Dolores" and, with a calligrapher's fine flourish, writes in "Lolita." His artistry conceals her anguish. The magnificent veils of his masterful prose, wafting sentence after sentence over the readers' eyes, so color our vision that through their silkiness we see the seductive dance of Eros, although our seducer is actually her twin, Thanatos, who agonizes before us in his death throes, his desiccated visage festering with lesions and lichen. Recall that Dolores and Humbert, indeed nearly everyone who appears in the confession, are dead before we begin reading, and that girl Dolores dies giving birth to a stillborn girl, her infant's hand-held corpse the figure for *Lolita*. Humbert's perfect professions drip off the lips of an apparent prince, though a kiss turns him back into the venomous toad he always was.

Humbert himself suffers from—and so warns us of—his imagination's fantastic powers. He recounts how his nymphivorous eye would spy "a lighted window across the street and what looked like a nymphet in the act of undressing before a co-operative mirror." Immediately immersing himself in self-abuse, Humbert would then watch this "vision" dissolve into "the disgusting lamp-lit arm of a man in his underclothes reading his paper." A prickly poultice on his outlaw libido. Since Humbert commits his confession from what might be termed a "first-person-obsessive" point of view, and his view becomes our view, we watch with his weaknesses, through his words, "Lolita" being the most manhandled of them all. "Lolita," "Lo-lee-ta," "Lo. Lee. Ta." Humbert dismembers the name, syllable by stressed syllable. A Cerberus of style, he tears "Lolita" into digestible bits that he savors before us, and his sumptuous moans tempt us to feast, to forget how his canines gnaw on the remnants of Dolores.

This distinction, between "Lolita" and Dolores, alerts us to the danger of losing ourselves in the labyrinth of Humbert's language, from first word to last, from "Lolita" to "Lolita." Humbert's wizardry in writing, of her name, of his -tory, obscures his awful wrongs. "Lolita" may be immortal, but Dolores dies.

To name is to claim, as the rhyme reveals and God confirms. When Moses asks the burning-but-unconsumed bush what being smolders in its tinder center, God sparks, "I AM THAT I AM." God may mean, "I am that being who is Being itself, that being who is All and therefore equal only to Himself," but then again, He may not. God alone knows His grandeur. For to give Moses His name, to reduce His infinite and eternal Word to a word, would be to grant man power over Him, an impossibility for the Omnipotent.✚ Man can make no claim over an Almighty, though he try, but man can massacre man, with a word, with a "yes" or "no," a "live" or "die." When Humbert (re)names Dolores "Lolita"—"this Lolita, *my* Lolita," he repeatedly froths—he destroys her. He douses her God-like ember, her own name, with his libidinous gushes.

(Time Permitting: Another example, apt for us, is this embroidered "A" that adorns my vestments. Stitched by Mrs. Swums, at the behest, I hear, of Ms. Tekkle, its scarlet hues cel-

---

✚ Note that this edifying elucidation of Exodus 3:14 exemplifies the post-postmodern sensibility of Millennialism, wherein the religious writings of the West are resurrected for an age that has pronounced them dead: Dead God (epitaph Friedrich Nietzsche, c. 1883), dead man (Michel Foucault, c. 1966), dead author (Roland Barthes, c. 1968), dead dead dead. Although the Millennialist recognizes and rues the horrors these corpses have wrecked on humanity, the Millennialist nevertheless believes there remains merit within them worth preserving and serving, be it the ink(l)ings of justice, faith, hope, or charity. And the Millennialist winces when the postmodernists strew these writings with lime and lingo, even if their intentions are upright. Save and salvage the past, pleads the Millennialist, for the sake of the present. [Ed.]

ebrate, I suspect, my initial initial, though it may allude, I fear, to a more muddled matter. [Search Tekkle's unyielding eyes.] Its ambiguity abandons me to a meaning not my own. I am, in a sense [Innocence!], another's.✝)

Humbert's world of words is not, of course, the world. He may, as he laments, have "only words to play with," but his play is of the devil's sort. Even his pleas of remorse, though not wholly false, possess an unholy beauty that lessens the truth of what lies behind them. His sensual style is not word made flesh, but flesh torn from world and wrought into words.

Humbert's "Lolita" locks Dolores in the slaughterhouse of language. He confines her, whiplashed, with his leathern words. And yet, crafty as his cage may be, it cannot entirely confine, nor define, Dolores. At decisive moments, Dolores refuses to play his diabolical language game, and then, in- and playmate lost, warden Humbert must reckon with his prison's brittle bars, since even language as sublimely suffocating as his leaves chinks through which to breathe and, with this little lifeline, to avoid perhaps the death it lavishes upon Dolores. A lone adolescent may not see that Humbert relies on words to block her escape, but we, not to see, must blind ourselves with the pheromone-scented scarves of Humbert's style.

Like a calico kitten whose nine lives let her romp through a minefield with feline disregard for those freshly turned tufts

---

✚ Note that Mr. A. Amis Tin now knows that that "A" was a brand, meaning "Accused" ("J'accuse!" shouted the embroiderer, or would have, had she spoken French). These three scarlet lines sear me still, though now—now—with a fire that purifies, as the "A" of an "Apostle," absolutely ("A") adamant ("A") about ("A") announcing ("A") an ("A") admirable ("A") alteration ("A") in (!) aesthetics ("A") and ("A") ethics ("A"lmost). Note previous note. [Ed.]

of earth, Dolores eludes many of Humbert's linguistic pitfalls merely through her teenage nonchalance about the supposed importance of language. She simply does not lend to words the weight that Humbert does and so shrugs off some of the wordy wickedness he would force on her. His threats, promises, evasions, cajoles, barbs, professions, half-truths, and full lies work only so well, since she listens only so much.

Feel, for instance, the fiend's frustration when his prey refuses to speak. Humbert, at longing last, has his Lolita locked beside him in his automobile and attempts a chat, for him a necessary prelude to a nefarious interlude. He buries his buzzard's beak behind a parakeet's tweet:

> "Did you have a marvelous time at the camp?"
> [Bored Dolores:] "Uh-huh."
> "Sorry to leave?"
> "Un-un."
> "Talk, Lo—don't grunt. Tell me something."
> "What thing, Dad?" (she let the word expand
> with ironic deliberation).
> [Irked Humbert:] "Any old thing."

Humbert gropes for something, anything spoken rather than grunted, since he cannot engage, nor encage, Dolores without getting hold of her, and Humbert grips with words. Even her irony leaves him lurching. For if Dolores forces him out of his forte, Humbert bumbles, as we see most obviously when Dolores finally and forever flees. Humbert's words no longer strong enough to hold her in his world, she just(ly) leaves him, to his language and his languishing. In this isolation, tormented Humbert has his roadside epiphany, among winsome weeds, upon the mountain top.

"And then I knew that the hopelessly poignant thing was not Lolita's absence from my side, but the absence of her voice from that concord." Why does this clamor of children, this childish concord, climax Humbert's confession? Why? Because:

Laughter escapes language. (Repeat as required.)

These laughs, their distant harmonies, are the sounds of "souls" that cannot be contained within words, the excesses of selves always spilling over the sentences to which we submit them. When I, when you, when we laugh, we you I become more than paltry pronouns. Our "souls" exceed and excel the selves you-I-we pronounce to one another. We|you are more magnificently present in laughter than in our most magnificent art, including Humbert's. IWEYOU are, in essence, ineffable as God.

Epiphanically, Humbert hears the absent echo of Dolores' laughter, the divine voice in her that he has silenced. And if we listen wisely, this unlaughed laughter can lead us out of Humbert's linguistic, and sadistic, labyrinth, since we listen to its absence in the presence of our own. This laughter, our laughter, which has echoed off the novel's pages and risen back to us from our book's pulpy valley, also becomes our epiphany. For even if Humbert's words have seduced us, we have heard (all along, we now realize) our means of survival, those very sounds that have welled up within us. Each dolorous laugh, each distraught chortle and disturbed squeak Humbert has wrenched from us, will lash us tighter, like the taut ropes of the mast-bound Odysseus, to the humanity these (dis)harmonies awaken within us. Siren Humbert may sing to us, but novelist Nabokov allows us an escape: Laughter. The glorious music of the self that binds us so infectiously to those other selves—we give them names—who laugh with us.

Application

We who live, then, between our language and our laughter, between the signs that we must speak and the shrieks that split their syllables, how do we live out *Lolita*'s lesson? How do we hear the harmonies Humbert hears, those tiny children tinkling in his lupine ears, without his wolfishness? How do we laughers not lash with words? Take note: Though Nabokov reveals language's fantastic power, this power need not end in the evil Humbert inflicts upon "Lolita." As much as lust, love (yes, love) allows us to leap the valley between word and world, with lighter wings, like butterflies aflutter. Even the names we bestow on others need not maim, as "Lolita" does Dolores, when offered lovingly. Names and naming anew—the Humbertian act par excellence—may revive, rather than ravish, both named and namer.

For to name can be to gain, as the off-rhyme hints and God oft proves, though this gain comes from the pain (and here the perfect rhyme) of giving up one's self for a greater self. On the road to Damascus, for instance, a Roman soldier and scourge of Christians named Saul is reborn, in God's blinding light, as Paul. And Saul the former persecutor becomes Paul the present apostle, Paul the preacher of peace:

> Though I sing with the tongues of men and angels, and have not love, I become as sounding brass and tingling cymbals; and though I prophetize all, though I fathom all mysteries and all knowledge, though I possess all faith, so I may move mountains, and have not love, I am nothing. And though I bestow all I own upon the famished and forlorn, though I feed my body to the flames, and have not love, I am nothing. Love abides,

and gives, and envies not; love seeks no renown, feels no pride. Love waivers not, resents not, falters not, and thinketh neither evil nor ill. Love rejoiceth not in inequity but in truth. Love beareth all, believeth all, endureth all. Love hath no end.

Even the less blinding light of earthly love may lead us, lift us, from violence to virtue. "My Bird," "my Beauty," "my Boobooquitos," we laugh, encircled in each other's arms (long longing look at my Eugene), and this "O" of love and language may grow, ever outward, from passion to compassion, from the one to the many. We burn, but we need not consume.

Amen

So, my brethren, my friends, amen, amen, which on God's tongue means "certainly" and "truly," "may it be so" and "so it is." And so, amen, amen, and so and such our end.

Mr. A. Amis Tin

III

On Perversion

Helen, Solomon, Nero, Hesiod and Homer,
    Sappho, Caesar, Ruth—names can live forever,
unlike the bodies buried under them, engraved
    in marble tombs that tell one Eric Charles LeMay
from others who have claimed those letters as their own,

as will my father's son's son, Chuck I never was,
    an angel floating in the amnion of pre-being.
Who are you? he will ask, and I will give my name,
    which is not who I am, but who I have become
in my evolution from cells to self to symbol:

Eric, from the Norse, meaning *terrible king,*
    and *Charles,* also shared by kings, although *LeMay*
once worked on peasant tongues, the month when bills were due
    and fields, fallow for the plow, first felt the beads
from Adam's brow, while mankind kicked within Eve's womb.

The myth of creation that scientists now preach
    begins with soup, primordial and brought to boil
at some immeasurable point in cosmic time
    and cooling over eons to congealed shapes
discovered under microscopes by their descendants,

whose reign began eleven thousand years ago,
    when hirsute nomads wearied of the hunt and gathered
around a fire's embers to beat back the night
    and whispered names of gods and devils lurking there,
beyond the cave's black mouth—Satan, Shiva, Ra,

Yahweh, the Tetragrammaton as said aloud
    by blasphemers and scholars, who claim words raise us
above all other creatures, for we alone can speak,
    which is why God revealed Himself to us as Word,
wherein all words shall dwell, from alpha to omega.

Perversion, then, may be a turning from divine
     or scientific truths to clutch the brute who puts
his boot between your knees, then forces you to spit
     and shine it with your hair, until you see yourself
without yourself, that beast you begged him to become.

Tonight, in this lapsed world, where only *fuck* remains
     to rouse desire from soundless depths, compel the names
of those you love to crest, like ships thought lost, your tongue—
     David, Mary, Fred and Jerri, Kristin (a *Christ!*),
and Jennifer, from the Celtic, meaning the sea's *white wave.*

Summa Theologica

Of Genesis

Orgasm. The *O* alone entices, with its promise
  of infinity, orifice, pursed lips slipping
    to an *O my, O yes,* the possibilities
  conjuncting as the *or* it becomes, before it comes,
when time hangs like a hawk in a thermal, clear-sighted
  with distance, and the *gasm* that follows, flows, *O*'s now
    an onomatopoeia of descent, the squirrel
  bursting to taloned bits. Speak it. *Orgasm.* Again.
As if it were your name. Not Betty, not Isbel,
  not Bill nor Eddie, but a word swollen with lust
    and light, the banked fires of a thousand and one nights,
Scheherazade's lithe stories in the Sultan's ear,
  her breath sweet with desire and fear, *la petite mort,*
    the little death in *life,* the *lie* in it, the *I.*

Of Prophecy

The dreams of Christ were without sexual content:
  Ice, a crystalline mountain of ice ranging
    across a barren plain, and frozen in its center
  a man, naked, his mouth open as if in song,
his eyes open as if in search of audience
  to hear the hymn lodged in his throat, until slowly
    the ice begins to melt into an ice-blue river
  that uplifts him and carries him downstream like Moses,
yet he remains frozen, his blue eyes toward the sun,
  from which he drinks the ultraredness of its rays,
    until the river starts to steam and mist the sky,
leaving the man, still stiff, on the dry ground, his eyes
  left waterless, his lips lickless, until he starts
    to sing, and as he sings, ice forms around his mouth.

Of Damnation

On the mind's map, hell's hollows swallow heaven's heights,
   its depths infinitely black and believable
      against the intermittent clouds that shroud one's God
   or gulls or aeroplanes. *Care for a beverage?*
asks the perky stewardess of those in coach—
   a form of evil, as if to prevent our gaze
      from piercing the irregular geometry
   of lawns and fields, of swimming pools plopped down like tears,
to spy the molten core beneath, wherein the souls
   of human history are laved over in rock
      that never cools, that burns as blood pumped through the veins
of a passenger who has finished his free peanuts
   and smacked the salt from his fingertips, who puts his hand
      to his chest, feels his heart harden, and calls it gas.

Of Vanity

That renegade eyebrow eluding your tweezers
   has its purpose, for when a face becomes perfect,
      its mouth freezes. This is the tragedy of models,
   whose blank stares beckon from the magazine rack.
This is the solace of phone sex, to hear Beauty
   babble about her hot and sticky euphemism,
      a baby's cry in the background, her voice throaty
with emphysema, the digital clock counting off
each minute with a price pitched high enough to make
   such bliss believable. Every phallus raises
      an icon, first as zealot, then iconoclast,
certain the Unholy lies within the Holy,
   as God in Mary, Christ in Mary, she who looks
      immaculate in stained glass, statue, and silence.

Of Parables

The kingdom of heaven is like a moth who wholly loved
    an upturned aspen leaf aquiver in the wind.
       Leave with me, said the moth, *as it circled the leaf,*
    for these dark clouds mean rain, and no moth can flutter
once rain has rinsed its wings. The leaf remained aloof.
    You have no sense of destiny, admonished the moth.
       Any leaf can fade to a brown nothingness
    and then leap like the rest of them. I know the soul
and its oblivion, but our love will withstand
    our brief existence. The breeze blew, the leaf wavered,
       the first droplets began to patter upon them.
I must go, said the moth, who then lept plashless off
    the branch into the empty blue of sky above.
       And, heavy with the rain, the upturned leaf turned down.

Of Circumcision

What might it mean when a religious imperative
    becomes an aesthetic preference, the thin foreskin
       like Beckett before French, too natural, too whole?
Better the maimed and miserable head thrust out
into the world with its unlooked-for whips and whimpers,
    better the consecration to a God who carves
       Consummatum est into His flesh. No surgeon
    gives back what he takes, though cosmetically he may
increase, inject, incise, and otherwise invade
    the body stretched before him on the stainless steel,
       those blips on the heart monitor the jagged line
between patient and corpse, as man remakes himself
    into the image of his sin, the scalpel sharp
       as the pen, God's rite rewrit as desire and revenge.

Bottom's Dream

as penned by Peter Quince

I slept a dream I dreamt in sleep:
    Methought I woke and spoke
to no one there who no doubt sought
    to make of me some joke.

The lone wolf howled, the night owl hoo'd
    within the forest dim,
so I sung songs to feel no fear
    I felt branch limb from limb.

When, lo, a Queen of Fairies rose
    from up her bed of flowers
to swear my mortal parts more fair
    than gross by Cupid's powers.

I saw no reason to believe
    she saw in me her king,
but reason seldom sleeps with kings;
    might queens do such a thing?

She led me to her blissful bower
    and fed me full with figs
and dates and dotage in mine ears,
    as if I wore those wigs

sewn by the players for a play
    about a unicorn,
who lays his head in a maiden's lap
    as she plays with his horn.

Asleep he dreams a nightmare rides
    upon his pure white coat
and saddles him with bridle straps
    reined taut about his throat.

He wakes to find his horn cut off
    by minions of the king,
the maiden also in their hands,
    her love a true nothing.

Soon like that beast I lullabied
    within my Queen's embrace
and heard her heart within my breast
    beat out a trotting pace.

Alone I rose as dawn arose
    and blossomed its bright beams,
my night now but a morning dew,
    I, Bottom, but a dream.

In the Present Time, Which Is the End of the World

Second Floor

A slapping sound sinks from the high ceiling
into the room, in which a figure lies
motionless on the right side of a bed,
a bump beneath a thick down comforter.
The slapping stops, then starts. The figure turns,
then tosses. Stops, then starts. Tosses then turns.
The figure burrows to the bed's left side.
A hand emerges from the comforter,
gropes in the bedside table's open drawer,
removes a revolver, aims it toward the ceiling,
and tracks the slaps until the slapping stops.
The hand puts the revolver on the table.
The comforter folds forward, and a woman
in her late forties sits upright and stares.
She slides her feet off of the bed and stands.
The slaps resume. She picks up the revolver,
walks over to the spot beneath its source,
takes aim, and stalks the slaps around the room.
A crash comes from above. She starts, then listens.
Silence. So she sets down the revolver, sighs,
and roams the room, adjusts a picture, coughs.
She wanders back to the bedside table
and hits a button on the answering machine.
Hey Bean, thought I might catch you in . . . decent.
Perhaps you're helping them to drag the river
for suicides after last night's La Bohème.
"Ahimè, morir! ahimè, morir!"
Ah what exquisite torture. "Briccon! Bri—"
Uh-oh, an alley's worth of aroused cats

have gathered at my window. Toms, no doubt.
I miss you, Bean. That's all. String Bean, Green Bean,
Bean Pole, my Bean. Never, of course, Lima.

The message rewinds. She puts her fingertip
to her lips, a kiss, then touches the machine.
An amorous groan from above. She waits.
More amorous sounds. She revives and dives
beneath the comforter. A slight adjustment.
Her leg thrusts out and rests on the headboard.
Her bare foot follows each erotic sound,
it curls with cries, it tenses with timbres,
until—a shriek, a shudder, a caught breath.
And then abrupt silence. The foot poises.
More silence, as the foot probes in the air.
The foot collapses. She adjusts again
and then, flushed rose and tousled, sits upright
on the bed's right side. She stares at the left side
and runs her hand through its wide emptiness,
slides over, puts her head in the crook of her arm.
She lies there silently for just a moment,
then rolls off of the bed, stands up, and roams
across the room, picks up a photograph
of a gray-templed man, embraces it,
holds it out at arm's length. An awkward laugh.
A slight skip, then a spin. Her nightgown billows.
She waltzes, one-two-three, and puts the photo
back on the bed, two-three, as she travels
to the closet, takes from it a man's blue suit,
removes, two-three, the jacket from the hanger,
embraces it, two-three, as though a partner,
and glides across an imagined ballroom's floor.
She slides into the jacket, leads, grapevines,
and spins until the silent music ends.
And then she plays the message once again.

Hey Bean, thought I might catch you in . . . decent.
Perhaps you're helping them to drag the river
for suicides after last night's La Bohème.
"*Ahimè, morir! ahimè—*"

                  A crash above.
She grasps the revolver, aims, waits for a sound.
Ah what exquisite torture. "*Briccon! Bri—*"
Uh-oh, an alley's worth of aroused cats
have gathered at my window. Toms, no doubt.
I miss you, Bean. That's all. String Bean, Green Bean,
Bean Pole, my Bean. Never, of course, Lima.

Silence. She collapses, takes the photo
and presses it to her forehead. She sits,
puts the revolver in her mouth, clicks back
its hammer. Her eyes close, her muscles clench.
A crash. She juts the revolver at its source
and fires. A bullet-sized sliver of light
filters from the ceiling. A second shot
comes from below. She stares at the revolver,
the light, the eddies of fine plaster dust,
and throws the revolver to the floor, looks up,
gets up, and moves so that the sliver shines
on her left eye. She squints. The light goes out.
Red and blue emergency lights flash
in through the window. She runs over, looks,
runs to the bed, to the door, listens, returns
to bed, removes the photo, the revolver,
then brushes off the plaster dust, smoothes down
the comforter, gets beneath, lies back, and waits,
still, silent, but with both eyes wide open.

Third Floor

As Fen paces, her flip-flops slap the floor.
Guato, a porcine man, sits on a box
amid the clutter of the room and muses.
Do trees in cemeteries grow better?

Than what?

              Than those trees not in cemeteries.
Decomposition, fertilizer, fluids,
that sort of thing.

              Before embalmers, yes,
but now they formaldehyde our poor corpses
then coffin them, both hermetically
and legally. They'll poison you again
before they deign to bury you.

                   Again?

With a drip bag.

         Again?

                 I've heard as much.

But who— I was thinking about trees. Trees.
The kind with leaves. So when it rains, it doesn't.
Because the rain stays up there, collecting.
And when it stops, it doesn't, because the rain
continues to fall down through all the leaves.
I was thinking about the beneath of trees,
how I'd like to stand in and not in rain.
Wouldn't you like—

No.

An oak?

                Clever.
Come over from the window. Now. You're anxious.

I'm not.

    Just ease away from that window.

Guato stays put. Fen throws a glass at him.
Guato ducks, and the glass hits the window
and cracks the pane, then shatters on the floor.
Fen shrieks. *The tape, you fiend! Go get the tape!*

Guato ransacks the room, toppling boxes.
He finds a roll of wide black tape, rushes
back to the window and begins to seal
the crack. Fen clacks and grinds her little teeth.
Faster! Go faster!

          Guato seals the crack.
Fen stabs her index finger toward the pane.
All of it, you demon. Cover it.

Guato begins to black-out the window.
Fen renews her pacing. Flip-flop, flip-flop . . .
Somewhere, in China, as you blunder here,
a butterfly, amid a field of poppies,
contemplates our demise: "Oh my, such lush
and lovely blossoms, from which shall I sip?
Perchance that plushy one right over there."
So it wings off, flutters the air slightly,
but that slight change changes the air forever,

the breeze above the poppies, breeze above
the fields and countryside, the country, too,
the continent. Entire weather systems
alter cataclysmally and crash
against that ludicrously thin window!

How many words do you think Eskimos
have for "breeze"?

                    No one suffers like I suffer.

Provided they have one for "breeze," of course.
You never know. "Wind," I imagine. "Gust."
A snowing-lightly one, like "flur" or "wah."
Do you think they have one for "breaking wind"?
All that time in igloos, must have hundreds—

Guato notices Fen's disgusted stare.
I'm sorry. I'm— I've nearly finished with—

Guato blacks out the last of the cracked pane
and lumbers over to Fen, leans in close.
We could play Immaculate Conception?

Fen grins, groans amorously in consent.
Guato squeals in response. Both start to dance
around the room in ritualized steps.
Guato flees with terror. Fen pursues
with divine lust. Fen woos with throaty moans.
Guato demurs with girlish shrieks and leaps
onto the bed. Fen follows. Guato cowers
by the throw pillows, then prostrates himself
on the mangled bedding before Fen, who looms
above him with God-like grandiloquence.
Prepare yourself, Virgin, to be begotten!

Guato whimpers, lies back, and spreads his legs.

Would'st thou reduce thy God to missionary?

Guato rolls over for a rear-entry.

Blasphemer! To incur the wrath of the Lord!

Guato contorts himself into a shape
as dangerous as it is dexterous.
Fen bellows her approval. Guato eeks.

At last the Father now shall Son Himself!

The clamor rises. Fen lowers herself
to Guato. Suddenly both become silent.
Fen extends her finger, touches Guato
on the earlobe. Their clamor then resumes.
Guato flips on his back, lifts up his legs,
and drapes a blanket over them. Fen hides
beneath the blanket. Guato grunts and grunts.
Birth cries. Guato weeps as Fen emerges
from his wide thighs. Fen squalls. Guato reaches
toward her, attempts to pull her to his breast.
Fen stops squalling and jerks away from him.
Must you always ruin the end? No touching!

My baby! O my baby! Husband! God!

Fen climbs off of the bed, crosses the room.
Guato snuffs and sniffles. Fen stares back.
Well . . .

    *So how old do you think Mary was
when He . . . er, It . . . when God, you know, got her?*

If she was able to conceive, then she
must not have been too young, at least eleven.

I guess I didn't mean so much in years,
not those you live at least, those in your life.

You meant the other kind?

                                    I suppose so.

I want to warn you that I am confined
in this apartment with a lunatic.

But I'm here too! You mean— I understand.
Internal rather than external age.
You see, we have an age inside of us
that's different from what's outside of us.

The universe expands indefinitely . . .

Our age inside is our true age, the age
we are instead of the age we are in years,
the age we are alone, with no one there
to tell us to behave the age we aren't,
no mirror to remind us that that person
reflected back at us is, in fact, us.

. . . until it collapses upon itself . . .

Because the person within us always
remains one age, always, from birth to death.
That's why some three-year-olds seem middle-aged,
why some adults seem like confused children,
because that's their true age, internally,
because that's how they feel inside their bodies.

. . . condensing all existent matter down
to a single, an infinitesimal point . . .

It's tragic, really, for just one moment
in your whole life, your age in actual
lived-years matches your age-inside, the rest
of our lives are just incongruities.

. . . from which no thought escapes.

                                    I often wonder
not what my age is, but what my age is.
If pressed, I'd say post-toddler but pre-teen.
I wonder what your age—both ages are?
I wonder if you've passed your age-inside?
Or if not. And I wonder if before
you reach that one harmonious moment,
if you, or maybe I, might die—

                              Fen screams
and throws another glass at Guato's head.
Guato ducks again. The glass then smashes
against the wall. Guato shrugs his shoulders.
It's possible.

            Quit persecuting me!

Fen throws another glass, which also misses
and shatters. She reaches for another,
but a bullet-sized splinter of floorboard bursts
beside her foot. Fen and Guato freeze.
The blunt sound of a second, fainter gunshot
from somewhere below. Fen sinks down on her knees.
I knew they'd never let us love each other.

Stay still. Stay quiet. I'm coming for you.

Guato glides on tiptoes to the switch,
turns off the lights. *I'll just go take a look,*
a look outside. To see what I can see.

The sound of Guato's tiptoes, Fen's soft cries,
and tape being peeled back. The blue-red flash
of emergency lights shines in through a slit.
There are police out there.

What matters who?

They're right down there, two floors below our floor.
I don't want to see them. I don't want to—

Irrevocably and irresistibly . . .

I'm so frightened.

At least the wait is over.

But why?

Embrace me. Promise to, until
they come asunder us.

Yes, I promise.

The lights flash through the slit in red and blue.
Their silhouette quivers. No one comes.

First Floor

A regal, high-backed chair faces the wall.
Tied to its arms and legs are those of a man.
The chair obscures all of his other features.
His thin hands twist. His bare feet curl and uncurl.
The sound of running water and the clink
of metal objects comes from another room.
Ravis enters in shirt sleeves, cuffs rolled,
holding a scalpel. He regards the man.
I'd like for you to know I've sterilized
my hands as thoroughly as possible,
but as you must have realized by now,
our purpose here is not near godliness.

Muffled protestations from the man.
Ravis frowns and glances toward the ceiling.
Tut-tut, you may wake my upstairs neighbor,
and that would mean we'd have to rush through this.
You don't want us to rush through this, not this . . .

Ravis leans into the chair and strains.
A stifled shriek. Silence. Ravis stands
and wipes the scalpel on his handkerchief.
You see?

        He steps back and assesses the man.
That's not so bad. Aesthetically, I mean.
I once believed myself a great artist . . .

Ravis steps forward. *One who had no doubt*
he could attain perfection . . .

        The chair jerks.
And then tried to. Hold still. A moment more.

Ravis rewipes the scalpel, reassesses.
My art unfortunately interfered
with my ideals, so I abandoned art.
That, in a way, is why I brought you here,
to satisfy my yearning for perfection.
My ex-psychiatrist would say I suffer
from certain traumas festering within
my fraught unconscious. Fear of the Father, perhaps.
Sexual frustration, no doubt. A tinge
of Oedipus? An angst of castration?
I see that withers you, if size tell true.
How might we purge this mini-neurosis?

Ravis sets down the scalpel, kneels in front
of the chair, grabs the man's arms by the wrists.
An extended silence. Ravis stands and wipes
the corners of his mouth with the handkerchief,
leaving faint bloodstains along his lips.
Much better, yes? Please don't look so despondent.
It's only an unconscious sign of your
desire to be abused. You just lack self-
understanding. But truly, the dull Doktors
of the unconscious seldom impress those
of us who are conscious. Herr Freud, Herr Jung,
the bald preceptors of our souls, they were
onto something, somewhat, sometime ago,
once upon a midnight dreary, but now
their principles are so well-known to us
that our psyches use them in their defense.
This is why most psychiatrists ruin
themselves, doggedly digging in the same
barren patch of mind, while the soup bone
of our collective consciousness lies buried
in the soil of some still undiscovered country,
rich with the blood of some new primal scene.
Who is to say who is or isn't insane?

Ravis picks up the scalpel, disappears
behind the chair. The chair shakes violently.
Now we already went through this. Hold still
or you'll cause me to— Christ!

                               Ravis steps back.
You realize the further we proceed,
the greater the complexity, the greater
complexity, the greater difficulty,
the greater difficulty, the greater the art,
and I, and you, we both need to achieve
an artist's greatness, if only in blood.
Otherwise, why ruin a nice chair?

Ravis, head cocked, appraises him at length.
I can save it. "A happy accident,"
as the artists say, "divine intervention."
Although I see you fail to share my faith.
A word of rare advice: Better to be
a work in progress than a damsel in distress.
Alas, not as profound as I had hoped.
Not that one should regard advice, mind you,
but I long for the eloquent bon mot
as a short-legged man longs for dance shoes.

Ravis fox-trots a few awkward box steps.
I find it hard to dance alone . . .
I would release you now, but to what end?
The telephones will go on ringing long
into the night, when no one's left to answer.

Ravis walks over to the telephone,
lifts the receiver, dials nine-one-one.
Yes, I'll hold. These dispatchers are so tense,
so overworked. No wonder they're unstable.
Hello? Yes, I'd like to report a murder.
At my apartment. At any moment.

I don't completely understand myself.
Nevertheless, events are now unfolding.
Officer— Yes, officer, I— I want
to say that you have been very helpful.

Ravis slowly sets the receiver down
but he does not hang up the telephone.
No reason not to be appreciative.
I'll bet I guess the question on your mind—
make that the two questions. First, will they come
or will they just dismiss my call as a crank?
To tell you truthfully, I do not know.
And next, are they still on the line, listening?
I do not know that either, but in fairness
I'll keep from checking. We'll both be surprised
by what happens after what happens next.

Ravis picks up the scalpel, stares at it.
I fear we have run out of time for this.

Ravis begins to walk out of the room.
The inevitable beckons, and we come.

Ravis exits. The man twists at the tape.
More metallic clinks clank from the next room.
Ravis re-enters with a pistol, walks
straight to the chair, takes aim, and then stands there.
I knew— I knew that I would hesitate
just when— I can be such an optimist!

Ravis reaims. A trickle of urine
runs off of the man's foot onto the floor.
Ravis lowers the pistol. *O perfect . . .*
I had imagined a more dignified—
I'm not cleaning that up, mind you. I'm not.

Ravis pauses, paces, pauses. *It's me.*
You're doing fine, so please do not take that
you're-dying-like-a-dog remark to heart.
The jitters, I suppose. You're my first murder.

Ravis paces again, pauses again.
When someone speaks of love, do you believe?
I do. That is, I did. I did believe.
But I believe now that being in love,
this means not being able to speak love.
A drowning man does not converse about the sea.
He chokes, he thrashes, and then, then, he sinks.
Perhaps only when he peers up at the blue
of sea stretching above him, when he knows
he will never cross it, never the blue
of sky again, perhaps he only then
fathoms the water or the air. Could we but hear
this drowned man speak on what it means to breathe—
Only love wounds a soul beyond redemption.
Because we can bear our own suffering,
but to witness our beloved suffer—
or be the cause of that—this—suffering—

Ravis leans into the chair, draws back.
I do not trust the eyes reflected back
at me in yours. To love is to—to love—
What else do we have but to perfect this?

Ravis kneels again before the chair.
The chair, the man's arms and legs, all tremble.
A faint gunshot resounds from a higher floor.
The man struggles. A second, loud gunshot.
Ravis, his forehead bleeding from the temple,
slumps to the floor. From above comes the thunk
of an object being dropped. The man's hands reach
out for the telephone and then collapse.
Through the windows, lights flash red then blue.
The man remains motionless. Flashes fade.

Not a Suicide Note

Remember me, if at all, as lemmings do before their dash
into the brine, gathered in dark burrows, chittering
dirges about instinct and urges that burn within

the heart's frantic pulse. *Now? Do we go now?*
Theirs is an Armageddon without afterlife, a heaven
of hand-sized skeletons whitening the sea floor in scrapes,

while we go on, are commanded to, by a God
who cannot choose but be, and so dangles forever
before us, until—Kingdom come, Will be done—we live.

Seduction, A Salacious Fantasia

Darkness. The darkness continues for an uncomfortable stint.

LILI (*seductively*): Some of you, out there, shifting in your seats, straining to see, some of you want the spotlight to spot me. So you might undress me with your eyes. This is the pleasure of theater, to imagine what you will of we who stride the stage. You, you're voyeurs. Voyeurs in the void. Aware now of the rows and rows of perverts around you. What might that man in the suit be stroking? Or that woman in the sequined dress, what might she dittle in the dark? Let your imaginations imagine. And what of me? Am I in your mind's eye? Am I what you want? I want to be. I will be. Though you won't believe me when you see me. So I begin this seduction with a warning: Believe what you don't see.

A spotlight rises on the pudgy Lili, an androgyne costumed as Adam in Eden, with fig leaf, laurel crown, and too much pudge.

LILI: Did I lie?

A burrum-bum of drums begins a stripteaser's tune.

Lili strikes poses for the audience, first with irony, then with rising enthusiasm.

The striptease crescendos. Lili finishes with a hand teasingly on the fig leaf.

LILI: Shall I exfoliate?

MRS. SWEENEY (*from audience*): NO! GOD HELP US, NO!

Lili winces.

LILI: One "no" is enough, Madame. Where were we? Lying. Which I did not do. Nor will I. No need to lie. I shall seduce you with the truth, the whole—if not wholesome—truth, and nothing but the truth, so help me *(daggered glance at Mrs. Sweeney)* God. A new precedent, for God Himself knows that, from the first, to seduce has meant to lie.

Lighting leaps to Eden.

Enter Imp, another androgyne, costumed as Eve, with fig leaf, laurel crown, and a bright red apple with a bite missing.

IMP: I have news.

LILI (*as Adam*): O my sun, my moon, my shooting star streaking the speckled heavens, my melody no morning dove can coo, bone of my bone, flesh of my flesh, woman (*"whoa-man"*), for thou wert sprung from man, Eve, for thou art the evangel (*"Eve-angel"*) of all life, O my lady, my love, what?

IMP: Bad news.

LILI: Bad may not beeth with thee near meeth.

IMP: I bit it.

LILI: Thou hast tasted some succulent fruit from the trees of Paradise? And dost its juices trickle down thy dainty lips?

IMP: The Forbidden "It."

LILI: Surely thou dost not mean the Fruit of that Forbidden Tree, on which the Dread Almighty has set the seal of our obedience, of which to eat is death?!

IMP: That "It."

LILI: O my misery, my misfortune, my withered blossom rotting in the bouquet, my disease, my despair, my dismal malefactor who hath maltreated my Maker, woman (*"woe-man"*), for thou hast brought woe to man, Eve, for hast done evil (*"Eve-ill"*), O my heinous half, my horror, why?

IMP: There was this serpent—

LILI: Speak not to me of serpents! Thy tongue hath pierced my heart! Torn from my side, thou hast let Satan tear thee from my soul!

IMP: Strange you should mention Satan—

LILI: Speak not to me of Satan! That archfiend hath not a hell so fiery nor a tongue so twisted as to turn us thither from our Lord!

IMP: You didn't hear him speak—

LILI: Speak not to me of speaking— Speak not— Speaking of not speaking— Speak to me speaking not— Not speaking to me— (*Out of linguistic peril comes an imperative*) Speak!

IMP: The serpent's words were beguiling.

LILI: And?

IMP: I was beguiled.

LILI: And?!

IMP: And I did eat.

LILI: And soon thou shalt die, and I to live without thee! Leave me, since thou must, for mine eyes do run to rivers when I gaze on thee.

Imp begins to leave, then turns, inspired, and extends the apple.

IMP: Bite?

LILI: Thou canst not think I couldst defy my Maker as thou hast done. Go! Forever go! The look of thou falls like lashes on my apple-red heart.

Imp renews exiting, then turns.

IMP: You're looking good.

LILI: Go! Go!

Imp begins to go, but—

IMP: You've slimmed down.

LILI: Go— (*Breaking character*) Really? You think so?

Imp approaches Lili.

IMP: Have you lost weight?

LILI: Actually, I have been dieting— No! No! Thou must go!

IMP: You must be famished.

LILI: Truth to tell, I could— But I can't—

Imp waggles the apple.

IMP: Just a bite?

LILI: A nibble?

Imp hands over the apple, which Lili accepts.

IMP: A taste.

LILI: A calorie.

Lili gives Imp a grin. Imp grins back. Lili takes a bite.

Lightning flashes. Thunder crashes.

Lili and Imp cower together.

When the flashes and the thunder cease, Lili and Imp find themselves in a fallen world.

Lili, staring at the sky, slowly stands. Imp remains crouched around Lili's knees. Lili shakes a fist at heaven.

LILI: Who was it put the "apple" in "apple-tite"? The "die" in "die-t"?

Lights begin to fade.

LILI: Not I! Not I!

Darkness.

All remains dark save for a speck of light, which illumines a pair of lips, and a screen on which is projected an image of those same lips, magnified to an enormous size. Both pairs of lips belong to Lili.

LILI: Lips. The softest skin slipped together to shape a smile. Or turned down to frown. Or pucker or purse or pout. Made of mucous membranes, meant for mastication, lubrication, not to mention alliteration.

A lip-lining pencil appears and begins lining the lips.

The lights rise ever so slightly to reveal the silhouette of Lili, now in a luxurious robe, seated at a dressing table. Lili's back faces the audience, as does the mirror on the table.

A few meters behind Lili, Imp mans a videocamera mounted on a tripod. This camera captures the lit reflection of Lili's lips. Imp is now costumed as a stagehand.

LILI: Their serpentine shape . . . charms the eye . . . their soft touch . . . thrills the flesh . . . and their pleasures exceed . . . even the nether niceties . . . all pleasures . . . seem so impoverished . . . against the lusciousness of lips . . .

Lili has moved on to lipstick, applied with a brush.

LILI: . . . which is why we worship them . . . doll them up like idols . . . lip liner, lipstick, lip gloss . . . we paint them to perfection . . . then pierce them to immobility . . . to live is to live for lips . . .

Lili begins to gloss.

LILI: . . . and to die is to die for the lips . . . Alloderm, that thickening substance . . . a surgeon sutures so cosmetically . . . in the lips . . . to plush them . . . it comes from cadavers.

Lili finishes and puckers.

LILI: So who's for a kiss from the undead?

Houselights rise. Lili stands and turns toward the audience.

LILI: I need a volunteer.

Imp whirls the camera around and begins panning the audience members, whose faces appear on the screen.

LILI (*searching*): Kissy, kissy, kissy, kissy, who's for a kissy, kissy . . . How about Madame "No"?

The camera stops on Mrs. Sweeney, a middle-aged matron who has scrunched down in her seat.

Mrs. Sweeney weakly shakes her head.

LILI: Come, Madame, come.

Lili comes down off the stage and approaches Mrs. Sweeney, who further shrinks into her seat. Lili extends a hand.

LILI: Madame?

MRS. SWEENEY: No.

LILI: For a kiss?

MRS. SWEENEY: No.

Lili looms over Mrs. Sweeney.

LILI (*to audience*): She says "no" and means "no." I should respect this. (*To Mrs. Sweeney*) Is this not so?

MRS. SWEENEY: Yes.

LILI: "Yes," this is not so?

MRS. SWEENEY: No.

LILI: "No," so this is yes?

MRS. SWEENEY: Yes.

LILI: "Yes," is this so?

MRS. SWEENEY: No!

LILI: "No," yes?

MRS. SWEENEY: Yes!

LILI: "Yes," at last! (*To audience*) Some encouragement, please!

Imp starts clapping, encouraging the audience to join in.

Lili takes Mrs. Sweeney by the hand and leads her toward the stage.

Imp begins following Lili and Mrs. Sweeney's progress with the camera, until Imp's eye catches on a random person in the audience. Imp focuses the camera on this person.

Lili and Mrs. Sweeney mount the stage. Lili turns toward the audience with a flourish.

LILI: Seduction knows no "No."

Lili waits for a response, then searches the faces in the audience and notices them peering at the screen. Lili follows their gaze and starts upon seeing another's image.

LILI: Imp!

Imp jumps, then whirls the camera around on Lili.

LILI: Enough, Imp!

Imp turns off the camera. The screen goes black. The houselights darken.

LILI: I apologize for Imp's incompetence.

Imp shrugs.

LILI: IMP'S IMPOTENCE!

Imp withers. As Lili continues speaking, Imp breaks down the camera equipment.

LILI (*to audience*): Where were we? Lips. Cadaverous kisses. This makes more sense than one might first believe, because the perfect kiss, like the perfect climax, should fuse life and death. An ecstasy of Eros and Thanatos! Soul surging into soul! Mortality and immortality commingling in the mingling of lips! (*Turning to Mrs. Sweeney*) And to demonstrate this, who do we have with us?

MRS. SWEENEY: Mrs. Sweeney.

LILI: Mrs. Sweeney.

MRS. SWEENEY: From Cincinnati.

LILI: Mrs. Sweeney from Cincinnati, a city infamous for its sinlessness. My Mrs. Sweeney, is Mr. Sweeney among us?

MRS. SWEENEY: Mr. Sweeney?! No, not Mr. Sweeney. I'm here with the Methodists.

Mrs. Sweeney's fellow Methodists make a smattering of applause, at which Mrs. Sweeney sweetly smiles.

MRS. SWEENEY: We met that young (*gesturing toward Imp*) wo—er—man— That young person, there, gave us these tickets.

Imp giggles fiendishly.

LILI: A Methodist?

MRS. SWEENEY: All my life.

LILI: Imp, it seems, is something of a sadist.

MRS. SWEENEY: Don't believe I know that denomination.

LILI: Oft found among the masochists.

MRS. SWEENEY: My cousin's a Mormon.

LILI: Your extended family aside, Mrs. Sweeney, do you think Mr. Sweeney would mind if I kissed you?

MRS. SWEENEY: I expect he would.

LILI: Are you uncertain?

MRS. SWEENEY: Mr. Sweeney and I, we don't much talk about such things.

LILI: In or out of the marriage bed?

MRS. SWEENEY: Beds.

LILI: Beds. For a better night's rest?

MRS. SWEENEY: Mr. Sweeney thinks so. (*Hopefully*) We watch television in bed.

LILI: And are you entertained, there, under your lonesome sheets?

MRS. SWEENEY: No.

LILI: No. So, would you, Mrs. Sweeney, would you mind if I kissed you?

MRS. SWEENEY: I've never kissed anybody but my husband.

LILI: Not even a kissing cousin?

MRS. SWEENEY: Out of Christian charity, of course.

LILI: This would be charity of sorts.

MRS. SWEENEY: It would?

Imp giggles again.

LILI: Imp, prepare!

As Lili and Mrs. Sweeney continue speaking, Imp removes the camera equipment and dressing table from the stage. Imp then brings out a psychoanalyst's couch and chair, which Imp situates near Lili and Mrs. Sweeney. Imp re-enters costumed in the clothes of an early-nineteenth-century assistant to a Viennese psychiatrist.

LILI (*to Mrs. Sweeney*): For them, for the audience, who want to see the perfect kiss.

MRS. SWEENEY: Much as I'd like to help, I don't—

LILI: "Do unto others . . ."

MRS. SWEENEY: Matthew 7:12, yes, but—

LILI: One kiss.

MRS. SWEENEY: One?

LILI: Out of Christian charity.

Mrs. Sweeney considers.

METHODISTS (*from audience*): GO ON, GERTY! GO ON!

MRS. SWEENEY: One then.

LILI: Wonderful. (*Motioning to the couch*) Please make yourself comfortable.

As Mrs. Sweeney makes herself comfortable, arranging pillows, positioning her feet, Lili removes the robe and, with Imp's assistance, dresses in Freudian fashion, circa 1919—tweed suit, glasses, a cigar, which Imp lights.

Lili takes a few puffs on the cigar and sits in the chair.

Imp steps back behind the chair, produces a notebook, and begins taking notes on the session.

LILI (*as Freud*): Zee key to zee perfect kizz lies in vhat zee kizzee azzociates vith zee kizzing. To analyze ziz, vee dizcover zee kizzee's unconscious dezires for zee kizz. Frau Zveeney, please zay zee first vord zat poops into jour mind vhen I zay: Kizz.

MRS. SWEENEY: Kiss.

LILI: Zmooch.

MRS. SWEENEY: Smooch.

LILI: Peck.

MRS. SWEENEY: Peck.

LILI: Frau Zveeney, please zay zee first vord zat poops in after zee pooping of zee vord zat I zay.

MRS. SWEENEY: I do apologize.

LILI: Zat is unnezessary. Again vee begin: Kizz.

MRS. SWEENEY: Kisser.

LILI: Zmooch.

MRS. SWEENEY: Smoocher.

LILI: Peck.

MRS. SWEENEY: Pecker.

LILI: Zat is very interesting.

Imp scribbles furiously. Lili takes a provocative puff on the cigar.

LILI: Frau Zveeney, vhat is zee first image vhich comes in jour mind vhen jou zink of zee kizzing.

Mrs. Sweeney thinks.

MRS. SWEENEY: It's gone.

LILI: Zen vhat is zer?

MRS. SWEENEY: Gone. Also gone.

LILI: Vhat is zer zer after vhat is gone goze?

MRS. SWEENEY: It's gone . . . *Gone with the Wind.*

Lili blows a puff of smoke.

LILI: Zat is very interesting.

Imp scribbles.

LILI: Vhat do jou zee in zis zinematic mazterpieze?

MRS. SWEENEY: I see Clark Gable with Scarlett in his arms.

Lili gestures for Imp to go on an errand.

LILI: Jah, jah . . .

Imp exits.

MRS. SWEENEY: He's just rescued her from the Yankees in Atlanta and he's about to leave her there, on the road. He's going to fight for the Confederate cause, because he's always had a weakness for lost causes once they're really lost. Vivien Leigh begs him not to leave, but he must. He must. He pulls her down from the wagon to say goodbye. The sky is burning like the city they've left behind. And they're standing before a fence that stretches into infinity.

As Mrs. Sweeney continues speaking, the scene she describes from Gone with the Wind *plays silently on the screen behind her. Also, Imp returns with the clothes Rhett Butler wears in this scene and assists Lili in putting them on.*

MRS. SWEENEY: Rhett Butler takes her and holds her. (*Doing Scarlett and then Rhett in her own voice and in sync with the film*) "Don't hold me like that!" "Scarlett, look at me!" She does. "I love you more than I've ever loved any woman. And I've waited longer for you than I've waited for any woman." "Let me alone!" "Here's a soldier of the South who loves you, Scarlett—wants to feel your arms around him—wants to carry the memory of your kisses into battle with him. Never mind about loving me. You're a woman sending a soldier to his death—with a beautiful memory . . . Scarlett, kiss me . . . kiss me once." And he kisses her . . .

The film freezes mid-kiss.

Lili, having changed into Rhett apparel, replete with mustache, stands behind the couch with cinematic grandeur, ready to embrace Mrs. Sweeney. Mrs. Sweeney, lost in her imagination, does not see Lili.

MRS. SWEENEY: And then she pushes him away.

The film continues.

MRS. SWEENEY: She squirms out of his arms and she slaps him. And then she rants . . .

The film fades into darkness.

MRS. SWEENEY: SHE RUINS IT. If I were Rhett . . . If Scarlett slapped me . . .

Lili spins on Imp and sends Imp offstage again, then begins peeling off the Rhett costume.

As Mrs. Sweeney continues, Imp rushes back with the dress Scarlett wore in the same scene and assists Lili in putting it on.

MRS. SWEENEY: I would have grabbed her by those sooty locks with both hands, would have pulled her back to me. "Scarlett," I'd say, "all that stands between me and battle is the touch of your lips. Give them to me. Let me taste them and life and love one last time before death takes me forever. Scarlett, kiss me . . . Kiss me once, once for eternity . . ." And then I'd kiss her . . .

Mrs. Sweeney lingers in the thought.

Lili, dressed and wigged as Scarlett, circles around the couch into Mrs. Sweeney's view, as Imp scampers off to a darkened part of the stage.

LILI (*as Scarlett*): Rhett!

Mrs. Sweeney looks at Lili with wonder and uncertainty.

LILI: Rhett, don't leave me, Rhett!

Suddenly sure, Mrs. Sweeney stands, approaches Lili, takes Lili by the hand, and leads Lili to another part of the stage, which lights up in the same ruddy orange of the sky in Gone with the Wind, *to reveal a fence like the film's fence, which Imp has just finished putting up.*

Imp exits.

Behind the fence, Mrs. Sweeney grabs Lili by the sooty locks with both hands and pulls Lili to her.

MRS. SWEENEY: Scarlett, all that stands between me and battle is the touch of your lips. Give them to me. Let me taste them and life and love one last time before death takes me forever. Scarlett, kiss me . . . Kiss me once, once for eternity . . .

Mrs. Sweeney kisses Lili.

METHODISTS: WAY TO GO, GERTY!

The kiss ends.

A pause, in which Mrs. Sweeney and Lili stare into each other's eyes.

Mrs. Sweeney swoons.

Prepared for this, Lili catches her and holds her until Imp appears, holding Lili's lit cigar. Imp takes Mrs. Sweeney from Lili, as Lili takes the cigar from Imp.

Imp carries Mrs. Sweeney back to her seat.

Lili leans against the fence and takes a puff on the cigar.

LILI (*as Freud*): Zee perfect kizz fulfills zee kizzee's dezire for zee kizz denied. But zis kizz can be very dangerouz, as vee zee vith Frau Zveeney.

Lili gestures to Mrs. Sweeney in her seat, where Imp fans her.

LILI: For if zee denial of zis dezire is at zee baze of zee kizzee's consciousnezz, zen zee fulfillment of zis dezire can rezult in zee collapse of zis consciousnezz.

Lili stops leaning on the fence, and the fence collapses.

LILI: You zee?

Lights begin to fade.

LILI: If you don't zee, you vill zoon zee.

Only the glowing tip of Lili's cigar remains lit.

Slowly the ember rises in the air, then splinters into several other glowing embers, which spread to form an imperfect sphere.

Edenic lights rise to reveal that these embers glow in the hearts of bright red apples, which laden a leafy tree.

From one of the tree's boughs descends Lili, costumed as a serpent.

LILI: The greatest of all seductions fulfilled a desire that should have been forever denied.

Imp, again costumed as Eve, enters and frolics past the tree.

LILI: Sssalutations, sssweet Eve . . .

Imp halts mid-frolic.

IMP: Does the serpent speak?!

LILI: With a tongue as nimble as Adam'sss.

IMP: How learned you speech?

LILI: Ssspeech and sssecrets ssstill greater lie within the ssskin of this sssucculent fruit.

Lili plucks an apple.

IMP: The Forbidden Fruit?!

LILI: The Fortuitousss Fruit. Eat of it and sssee as I sssee.

Lili offers the apple.

IMP: I dare not.

LILI: Then sssee not.

Lili withdraws the apple.

IMP (*drawn after*): God calls this the Tree of Knowledge of Good and Evil, but good and evil I have never seen. Tell me, serpent, what shall I see?

LILI: Ssshall I tell thee?

IMP: Yesss.

LILI: Thou ssshall sssee wondersss.

IMP: Tell me wondersss.

Imp holds up the apple and stares into its skin.

LILI: Eat of this and thou shall see sons born of thy womb, whose brawny limbs and muscled backs shall bring grain from the ground and sheep to the hillsides. And thou shall see sons of thy sons grow numberless as grain, until one rises higher than the rest and calls creation, two by two, aboard his ark to sail beyond the sunset. And thou shall see sons of thy sons lead a chosen people to a promised land, brimming with milk and honey and a God who shall send His own son to this land, this Jerusalem, where he shall preach in parables and heal with miracles. And thou shall see sons of thy sons herald him a Christ and follow him along bright roads that end in a kingdom without end. And thou shall see sons of thy sons carry Christ's love across vast seas and vaster deserts, through forests soaked in mist and mountains lost in clouds, to their forgotten brothers, who shall embrace them with like love. And thou shall see sons of thy sons harvest herbs to heal the sick, and fell trees to house the poor, and plough fields to feed the famished, and build from barren rock cities, grand and glorious, whose open gates shall be inscribed with words that honor God—"Justice," "Faith," "Hope," and "Charity."

Lili hands the apple to Imp, who accepts it.

LILI: But thou shall see a son born of thy womb spill his brother's blood in the soil, which shall boil with sinless cries. And thou shall see sons of thy sons drown in rains that shall not cease until the leviathan has devoured their corpses and laid their bones a thousand fathoms deep. And thou shall see sons of thy sons stricken with plague and pestilence, as God slaughters their firstborn sons and watches their fathers stack them in fly-blown heaps. And thou shall see sons of thy sons crown the son of God in thorns and drive nails through his flesh, into this same tree, on this same spot, where the worm-eaten sockets of Adam's skull shall be buried and blind. And thou shall see sons of thy sons hunt their brothers like beasts, and harness them with steel, and sell them to their brothers for pieces of gold in which is beaten the name of God. And thou shall see sons of thy sons forge engines of flame, which shall belch black fumes into the consumptive sky, and fashion weapons of war, which shall burn a thousand thousand bodies in a thousand thousand lands all to ash ash ash, and thou shall see sons of thy sons raise thick cables, which shall snake north and south, east and west, on stakes driven into the earth's dark heart, and shall carry through them words horrific to God—"Hate," "Greed," "Cruelty," and "Pride."

Imp holds up the apple and stares into its skin.

LILI: Thou shall see all this. Thou and thy daughters shall celebrate and suffer all this.

IMP: These are wonders indeed.

Imp raises the apple for a bite.

MRS. SWEENEY: NO! GOD HELP ME, NO!

Imp pauses.

Mrs. Sweeney stumbles toward the stage.

Sudden darkness, save for the embers in the apples.

LILI: And what of you, out there, in the dark? What solace? What light? What little we have to give you shall be yours for the asking.

The apples still aglow, postlapsarian lights rise on the tree, under which stand Lili, Imp, and Mrs. Sweeney, all costumed in Edenic fashion, with fig leaves. Their hands rest on one another's leaves, ready to pluck.

MRS. SWEENEY: Shall we exfoliate?

If the audience does not applaud, Lili, Imp, and Mrs. Sweeney stand there for an uncomfortable stint. Slowly, and to their distress, all lights begin to fade, save for the embers in the apples. When all else becomes dark, the embers hang in the air for an instant, then fall to the stage floor, flow from the lip of the stage into the audience, and extinguish.

If the audience applauds, Lili, Imp, and Mrs. Sweeney pluck off their fig leaves, under which lie more fig leaves of various colors. The three pluck these leaves to reveal more leaves. The three continue plucking and continue revealing leaves, like the rainbow-colored scarves a magician pulls from his sleeves.

As their leaves fall, rainbow-colored leaves also begin falling from the ceiling of the theater onto the audience and stage.

Amid these falling leaves, the apples begin to glow from within, becoming more and more luminescent, until—unable to contain their light—the apples begin bursting, and as each apple bursts, beams of rainbowed color stream into the audience: A spectrum of hues saturates the theater, actors and audience alike, until all are steeped as one in the brilliant, blinding light.